The activities in this book are designed to help both children and their families become more aware of the importance of math in their everyday world.

- Collect books from your school and public libraries that show math being used in some way. (See bibliography on page 112.)

- Plan field trips where students can see math in action. For example:

  1. Plan a walking trip around the neighborhood to look for numbers (street signs with numbers, addresses on houses and mailboxes, license plate numbers, etc.).

  2. Plan a walking trip to look for geometric shapes on the homes around school.

  3. Plan a trip to a home for a counting "tour." Prepare children (in pairs or small groups plus an adult) with counting assignments such as "Count all of the light switches" or "Count all of the windows."

- Invite parents to the classroom to share a variety of ways in which they use math. Provide parents with guidelines so that their presentation is age-appropriate.

  1. cooking (measurement, counting, time, money)

  2. building something (measurement, counting, money)

  3. sewing (measurement, counting, money)

  4. games and sports (time, counting, writing numerals)

  5. personal finance (money, computation skills)

  6. how clocks help me (wake up, be on time for work or school, know when my favorite t.v. shows come on, etc.)

Arrange an area to hold center activities involving real math skills. Store activities in boxes, folders, envelopes, or gallon plastic bags.

You may choose to put out several different center activities at a time or to put out only one activity and change it frequently.

Plan some centers with individual tasks and others designed for partners or small groups.

Pages 3–6 contain center ideas and patterns. Many of the other activities presented throughout this resource book can be placed in centers as well.

Deliver the Mail (identify and match numerals)

Reproduce the house patterns on page 4. You will need a set of house pictures and some letter envelopes. Write house numbers on the houses and corresponding numbers on the "mail." (Use numbers from your students' addresses.) Place these in the center. Children read the envelopes and match them to the correct houses. If you have a large class, divide the houses and envelopes into two or three sets.

Piggy Banks (count pennies)

Reproduce the piggy bank pattern and amount cards on page 5. (Fill in appropriate amounts.) Provide a coin purse of pennies for the center. Children take turns drawing a card and then counting pennies into the bank to equal that amount.

Where Does It Go? (sort)

Reproduce two copies of the house cut-away on page 6. Post one copy at the center. Cut apart the rooms on the second copy. Glue each room onto a small box or box lid to be used as a sorting tray.

Place copies of an assortment of magazines and catalogs containing house furnishings, and scissors in the center.

Children are to find items that belong in each room (set a number in advance), cut them out, and place them in the correct room.

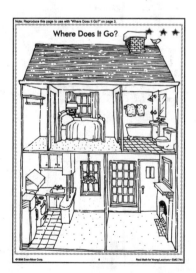

Note: Reproduce these patterns to use with "Deliver the Mail" on page 3.

Real Math for Young Learners • EMC 744

Note: Reproduce this page to use with "Piggy Banks" on page 3.

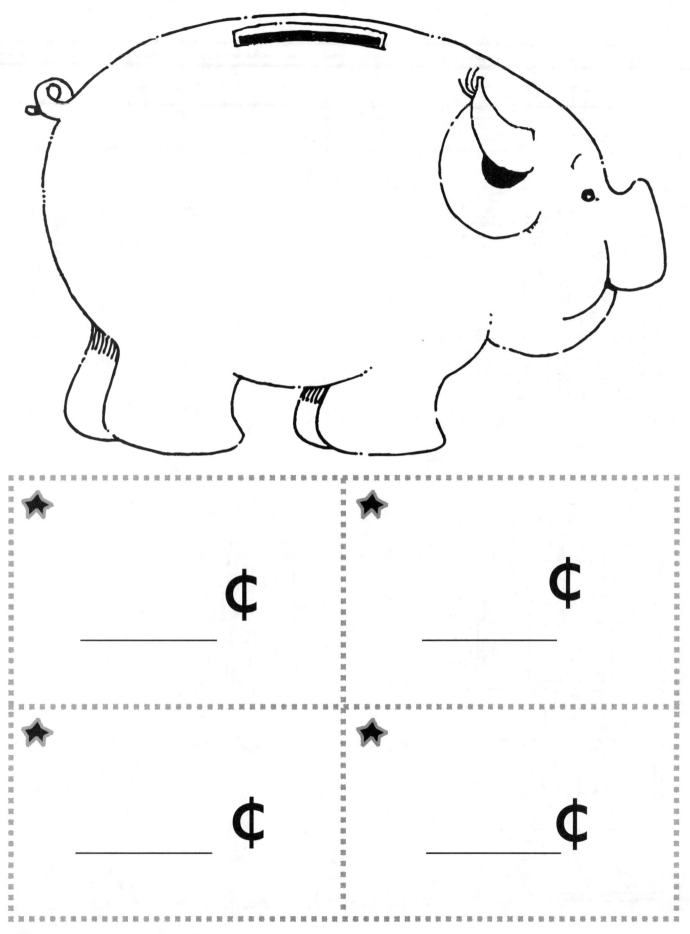

¢

¢

_____

_____

¢

¢

_____

_____

 Real Math for Young Learners • EMC 744

Where Does It Go?

6

Make the outside and the inside of a house as described below.

Materials:
- butcher paper in several colors
- black marking pens
- yardstick or meter stick
- scissors
- stapler

Directions:
Involve your students as much as possible in the construction of the two boards. Have them help you measure, draw, or cut out the pieces of the house.

 Outside of the House

Lay the butcher paper on the floor. Begin the house by making a large square out of one color. Lay a second color of paper along one edge. Cut a triangular roof. Using your remaining colors, cut five square windows, a large rectangle for a door, and a smaller rectangle for a chimney. Outline each piece with a black marking pen. Staple the pieces to the bulletin board. Lable the house "Outside."

Use this house to practice geometric shapes, counting, positional words, and size comparisons. Ask questions such as:

   "How many different shapes do you see?"

   "How many (triangles, etc.) do you see?"

   "Are there more rectangles or more squares?"

   "Where is there a triangle?"

   "How many windows are above the door?"

Lay out butcher paper and make a large square for the house and a triangle for the roof. Cut out a chimney. Use a black marking pen to draw the rooms in the house. Label the rooms as shown. Staple the pieces of the house to the bulletin board. Label the house "Inside."

Place pictures of furniture, other objects, people, and pets in the rooms. These can be cut from magazines and catalogs or drawn by you or your students. Change the pictures often.

Use this house to practice counting, positional words, and to make size comparisons. Ask questions such as:

"What room is above the kitchen?"

"How many rooms does this house have?"

"What room is the (largest, smallest)?"

"What room is between two other rooms?"

Graphing

Graphing as a Problem-Solving Tool

Many suggestions for graphing experiences are presented in this resource book. Graphing is a vital tool for mathematicians. It develops naturally from sorting and classifying activities.

Young learners enjoy comparing groups of objects. These simple comparisons **are** beginning graphs. They enable the students to make rough estimates of which group has more and which has less.

As students become skilled in graphing, the actual graphing becomes a way of organizing information and seeing relationships.

Graphing experiences should begin with real graphs and progress through picture graphs to symbolic graphs.

Real Graphs

If your class is not familiar with graphing, begin graphing with concrete objects— these graphs are called real graphs.

Start by comparing only two or three items on a floor grid. (See page 10.)

Picture Graphs

When students interpret real graphs easily and seem comfortable with them, substitute pictures for the real items. These graphs are called picture graphs. Students should be able to compare four and five items at this stage.

Our Shoes			
6			
5			
4			
3			
2	👞		
1	👞		
0	laces	slip-ons	indoor

⭐ Symbolic Graphs

Finally move to the use of a symbol instead of a picture or the real item. These graphs are called symbolic graphs. Gradually increase the complexity and the abstract nature of the graphs you make.

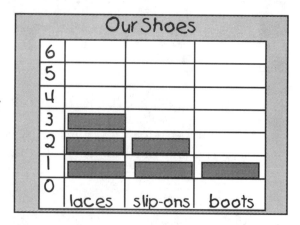

Our Shoes

	laces	slip-ons	boots

⭐ Interpreting Graphs

When your class has made a graph, always analyze and interpret the compiled information. Ask questions such as:

Which has the least?
Which has the most?
Are there more _____ or more _____?
Are there less _____ or less _____?

How many more _____ are there than _____?
How many less _____ are there than _____?
How many _____ are there altogether?
Are any of the items the same?

As your class becomes more and more familiar with graphing, simply stand back and ask:

"What can you tell me about this graph?"

Be ready to graph any time. Your students will suggest opportunities as you move through your school day. Take them up on it.

Save the graphs that you make. The students will enjoy referring back to them and will point out new information as their interpretation skills improve.

⭐ Using A Floor Grid

Suggested activities in this book sometimes call for a floor grid. To make the grid, use an old window shade or a piece of canvas. Paint or use a thick permanent marker to draw a basic grid pattern. When you want to make a real graph on the floor, roll out the floor grid.

Place the items to be compared on the grid, one in each square, just as you would if you were making a picture graph or a symbolic graph. When you are finished, roll the graph up until you need it again.

Numbers Everywhere

Help students to realize that numbers are a part of their everyday lives by searching for places that numbers and math are used at school and at home.

First do a "math search" in the classroom. Have students look for numbers and examples of ways math is used. Pose the challenge in the morning. Then in the afternoon record what the students found on a chart. Send a group of students with an adult helper to search out math in other parts of the school.

Next, send your students on a "math search" at home (house, garage, and yard). Have them look for places where numbers are used. Have them learn ways in which people in their family are using math at home.

Reproduce and send home the parent letter and record sheet on page 12 for students to use as they do a home "math search." When the completed student record sheets have been returned, compile a list of all the different places children found math being used in their homes.

Reproduce the activity sheet on page 13. Have students circle all of the places they see numbers or math being used.

Our School Math Search

number 6 on our door

number 8 on Mrs. Kim's door

numbers on clock

numbers on the telephones

a cookbook on the shelf

calculators

money to buy lunch

score in games

counting by 5s

numbers on the calendar

number on Joe's t-shirt

Math at My House

Dear Parents,

Help your child find the places around your house, garage, and yard where numbers are used. Your child may draw or write the answers or tell the answers as you write.

Please return the record sheet by _____ .
                                                    date

Thank you for your help.

I found numbers in these places:

My name is _____ .

My name is _____.

Using Numbers

13

Shapes Everywhere

Recognizing geometric shapes is an important early math skill. Help your students to notice these shapes in objects in their home and school environments.

Shapes in the Classroom

1. Cut several construction paper samples of each shape you intend to practice.

2. Hold up each shape and ask your students to name the shape and to tell how many sides and corners it has. Then have students look around the room and try to find something that has that shape. When a child sees something of the correct shape, have him/her raise a hand. Select one or more children to name what they have found. Hand the child/children the construction paper shape. Repeat with each of the shapes you are practicing.

3. Make a picture graph to show what shapes were found. Draw a circle, square, etc. on a chart. Have each child holding a shape put it next to the same shape on the graph. Count the number of each shape and ask questions that compare the number found.

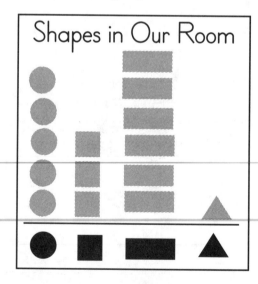

Shapes at Home

1. Explain to your students that now they are going to go on a shape hunt at home. Prepare for the search by asking them to think about shapes they recall seeing at home. Then brainstorm and make a list of these shapes. Guide the discussion by asking students questions such as:

    "What kind of circles do you see in the kitchen?"
    'What circles do you see when someone is sewing?"
    "What circles are in the garage?"

2. Repeat the activity, asking students to recall other shapes they have seen around the house and garage.

3. Reproduce the form on page 15. Explain to your students how to fill out the form as they look for shapes at home.

Math at My House

Dear Parents,

Help your child find geometric shapes around the house, garage, and yard. Your child may draw or write the answers or tell them as you write.

Thank you for your help.

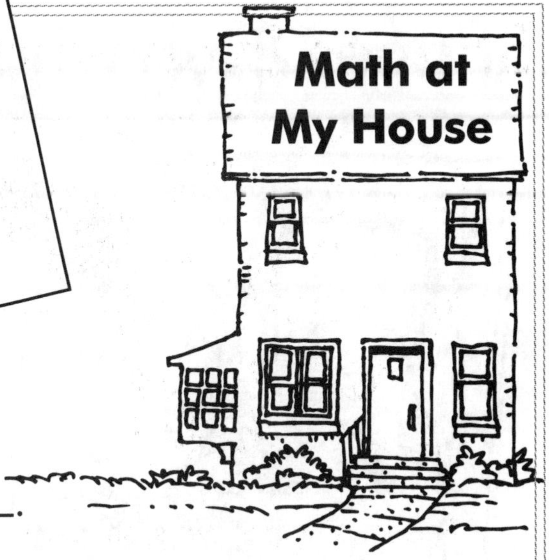

My name is _____.
I found these shapes at home.

circles

squares

triangles

rectangles

Math and My Family

Big and Little Families

1. Discuss how families come in different sizes. Some families are very small. Some families consists of many people.

2. Recite the clapping rhymes on page 19 together. Then ask students to think about the people in their home. Ask this question: "Do you have a big family or a little family?"

3. List student names and have each make a tally mark for each person in the family. Show students how tally marks can be made in groups of five.

Sue ||||

Carlos ⌶⌶⌶

Megan ||

When everyone has had a turn, have the class count each set of tally marks with you. If appropriate, have each child write the numeral after his/her set of tally marks.

Use the list to compare family sizes:

"Which family is largest? smallest?"
"Which families have the same number of people?"
"Are there more or less people in Sue's family than in your family?"

Use the list to do simple computations:

"How many more people are in Carlos' family than in Sue's?"
"How many people would be in Sue's and Megan's families if we put them together?"

Count Your Whole Family

Explain that we have more people in our family than just the people living with us in our house or even in our town. Explain the record sheet (page 20) they will be taking home. With their parents help, they are to make a list of all their living relatives.

Model the activity by putting your own family list on the chalkboard including yourself, your spouse, children, parents, grandparents, aunts, uncles, cousins, etc.

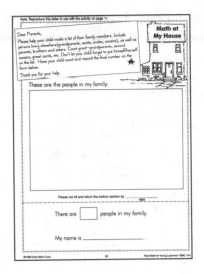

Graphing Family Sizes

Use the information on the family-size record sheets to create a bar graph.

1. Take a long sheet of butcher paper. (Size will depend on the number of pupils in your class.) Use a wide-tipped black marking pen to line the paper to form the structure of your graph (see sample). Write your students' names in a row across the bottom.

2. Cut lots of one inch (2.5 cm) squares of construction paper. Have each child read the number on his/her record sheet and count out that many squares to bring to you. Glue the squares in a column above the child's name on the graph. (This is a time-consuming process if you have a large class. Enlist the help of an older student or a parent volunteer to assist one child at a time to glue on his/her own squares.)

3. Use the completed graph to practice reading material from a graph, to make comparisons among the families, and to create counting and computation questions.

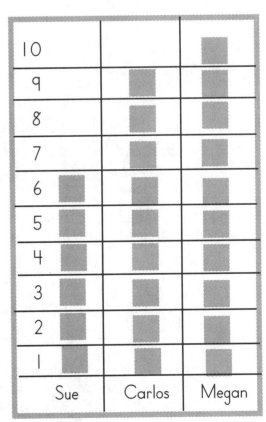

Tallest? Shortest?

Ask students to think about the size of people in their own families. Ask "Do you know who is tallest and who is shortest? How do you know? Can you think of a way to find out for sure?"

1. Demonstrate how to measure someone's height using a piece of string.

   Select three students to measure your height: one to tape the end of the string at the top of your head (you will need to lie down for this!) and one to hold the string at your feet (remind the student to pull the string taut). Have the third student cut the string at your feet.

   Pin the piece of string on a bulletin board with the bottom of the yarn just touching the floor. A piece of tape at the bottom will help pull the string straight.

2. Divide students into groups and let them measure each other. Pin the pieces on the bulletin board. Attach name labels.

3. Use the information on the graph to discuss how people are all different heights. Have children see if they can find two strings that are the same length.

4. Reproduce page 21 so that students can measure their family members. Compare information when papers are returned to class.

Note: Teach these rhymes to your students with the activity on page 16.

Family Clapping Rhymes

Reproduce the rhymes on an overhead transparency.
Teach the rhymes and have children clap each time they say a ★ marked syllable.

A Big Family

Fa - ther and Mo - ther
Sis - ters and bro - ther
Two grand - fa - thers
And one grand - mo - ther

Wait!
There's more!

Lots of Aunt - ies
Lots of Un - cles
Cou - sins, cou - sins
By the do - zens

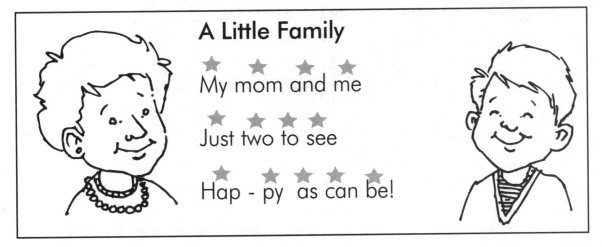

A Little Family

My mom and me

Just two to see

Hap - py as can be!

Real Math for Young Learners • EMC 744

Note: Reproduce this letter to use with the activity on page 17.

Dear Parents,

Please help your child make a list of their family members. Include persons living elsewhere (grandparents, aunts, uncles, cousins) as well as parents, brothers, and sisters. Count great-grandparents, second cousins, great aunts, etc. Don't let your child forget to put himself/herself on the list. Have your child count and record the final number on the form below.

Thank you for your help.

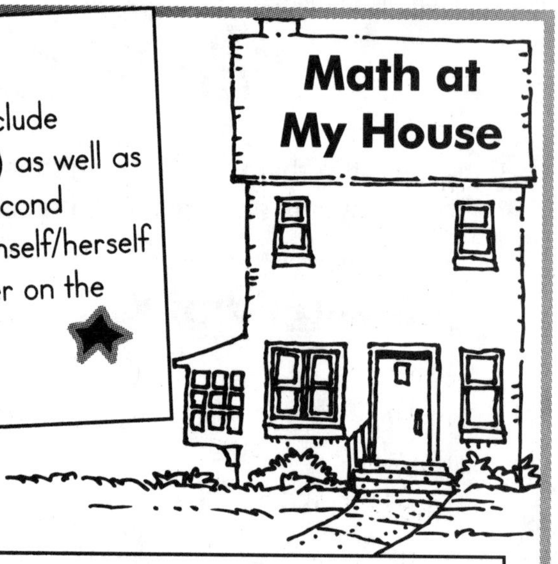

Math at
My House

These are the people in my family:

Please cut off and return the bottom section by ________________.
date

There are ☐ people in my family.

My name is ______________________.

Note: Reproduce this letter to use with the activity on page 18.

Dear Parents,

Please help your child do the following measuring job. He/She will need string or yarn, scissors, paper for name tags, and tape.

1. Have each person in the family take a turn lying down so your child can measure his/her height with the string. Cut the string, tape a name tag to one end and place it aside as the rest of the family is measured. Measure your child so he/she is included in the next step.
2. Lay all of the strings in a row with one end of each string even with the others.
3. Help your child write the names in size-order, with the tallest person listed first and the shortest person listed last.

Thank you for your help.

Math at My House

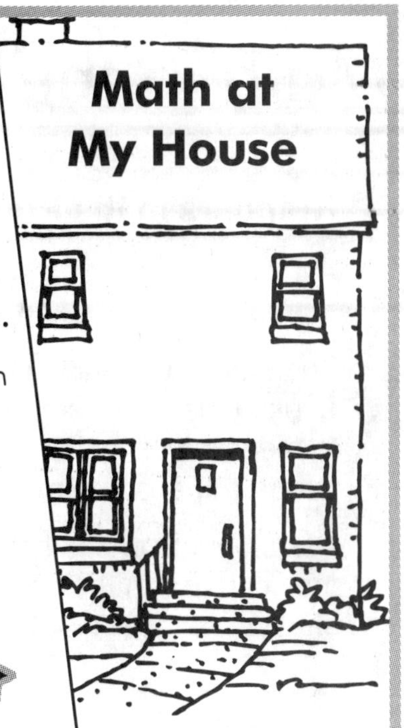

_______________________'s Family

Tallest _______________________

____

____

____

____

____

Shortest _______________________

My name is _______________________ .

Please return this paper by _______________ .

Math in the Kitchen

Numbers in the Kitchen

Ask students to think about places they have seen numbers in the kitchen. (Have samples available to share.)

Then ask students to describe how the numbers are used. Explain that most of the numbers found in the kitchen help to measure things. Some measure time, some measure temperature, some measure amounts of things.

Ask students to see how many of these measuring tools they can find in their own kitchens. Reproduce the record sheet on page 23 for them to mark as they find items.

> clock
>
> timer
>
> measuring cups
>
> spoons
>
> kitchen scale
>
> thermometer
>
> stove and oven

Counting to 100

The kitchen contains many items which can be used to count to 100 (dried beans, Cheerios, toothpicks, etc.).

1. Divide the class into partners. Give each pair a bowl with the item to be counted and a sheet of paper divided into ten boxes.

2. Have the students place ten objects in each of the ten boxes. Then go back and touch each object as they count from 1 to 100.

3. When everyone has their sets of ten counted out, explain that there is a quick and easy way to count the objects. Touch each box and count by 10s. Repeat this with the students in each group counting along with you. Then have the students count by 10s alone.

The activity can be repeated using other objects commonly found around the house and garage (buttons, pennies, nuts and bolts, etc.).

Note: Reproduce this letter to use with the activity on page 22.

Dear Parents,

Today we learned about some of the ways people measure things in the kitchen. Please help your child search the kitchen to find some of these measuring devices. Ask your child to name the item and tell what it is used for. If your child doesn't know, you can provide its name and demonstrate how it is used.

Your child is to color each item below found in your kitchen and to put an X on the items that are not found. Thank you for your help.

Math at My House

Measuring in the Kitchen

Color the things you find in your kitchen.
Put an X on the things you do not find.

★ Let's Cook ★

Cooking experiences are a motivating way to see math at work. Whether you cook with the whole group or have individuals create their own snacks, use the picture direction cards on page 25-27 to help students follow these three recipes step by step.

Chocolate Milk

Supplies:
- plastic glasses
- plastic spoons (for stirring)
- measuring cups
- tablespoons
- non-fat milk
- chocolate syrup

1. Put 1 cup (237 ml) of milk in a glass.
2. Put 2 tablespoons (60 ml) of chocolate syrup in the glass.
3. Stir 10 times with a spoon.
4. Drink.

Ants on a Log

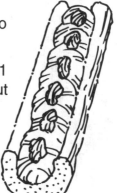

Supplies:
- celery
- peanut butter
- raisins
- tablespoon
- ruler

1. Cut celery stalks into 4" pieces.
2. Fill each piece with 1 tablespoon of peanut butter.
3. Add 6 "ants" to the log.
4. Eat and enjoy.

Fruit Salad

Supplies:
(substitute any seasonal fruit)
- green grapes
- banana slices
- cantaloupe chunks
- yogurt
- bowls
- stirring spoons
- knife
- cutting board
- eating spoons

1. In a bowl combine:
   3 chunks of cantaloupe
   4 slices of banana
   5 green grapes
   1 spoon of yogurt

2. Stir and eat.

Note: an adult should do any cutting requiring the use of a sharp knife. You may want to precut fruit into sizes that children can then cut with plastic knives.

Let's Make Chocolate Milk

1

Pour 1 cup milk.

2

Add 2 tablespoons of chocolate syrup.

3

Stir 10 times.

4

Drink - Yummy!

 Real Math for Young Learners • EMC 744

Let's Make Ants on a Log

1

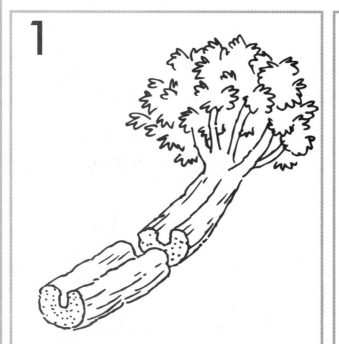

Cut celery into 4" log.

2

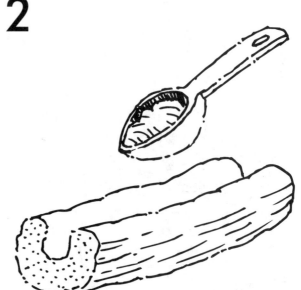

Fill celery log with 1 tablespoon of peanut butter.

3

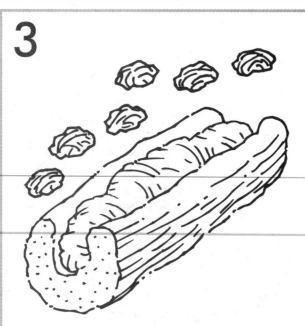

Add 6 "ants" to your log.

4

Eat and enjoy!

Cut your celery this long.

1 inch	2 inches	3 inches	4 inches

Real Math for Young Learners • EMC 744

Let's Make Fruit Salad

1

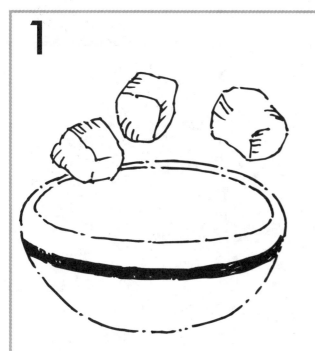

Add 3 chunks of cantaloupe.

2

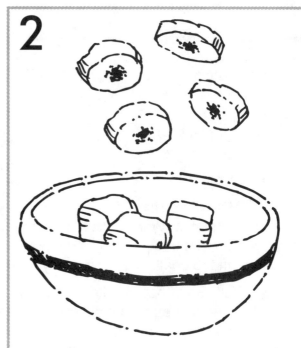

Add 4 slices of banana.

3

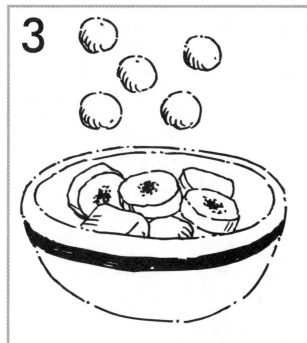

Add 5 green grapes.

4

Add 1 spoon of yogurt.
Stir it up and eat!

Popcorn Math

Teach your students the poem on the right as you are popping corn to use in the popcorn activities below.

Materials:
- electric popcorn popper
- popcorn kernels
- kitchen scale
- measuring cup
- several clear plastic cups
- kitchen scale

Making comparisons:

1. *Which Takes More Room?*
   Ask your students "Which takes up more room — unpopped or popped popcorn?" Record student answers on the chalkboard using tally marks.

   Place a half cup of popcorn kernels in one of the plastic cups. Pop the same amount of kernels. Take the popped corn and place it in as many plastic cups as necessary. Have students count how many more cups the popped corn took than the unpopped corn.

2. *Which Weighs More?*
   Ask your students "Which weighs more — unpopped or popped popcorn?" Record student responses.

   Place the popped corn on the scale and record the weight. Do the same with the unpopped corn.

Put in the oil.

Fill up the pot.

Plop go the kernels.

Now, wait till it's hot.

Pop goes the first kernel.

Pop goes the next.

Then pop, pop...explosion.

There go all the rest!

Linda Holliman

Estimating

Reproduce the popcorn record sheet on page 29 for each child. Show a cup of popped corn. Ask "How many kernels of popcorn do you think are in this cup?" Have students write (or dictate) the number on their "popcorn paper." Have a student take each kernel out of the cup, one at a time, as the rest of the class counts. When all the kernels have been counted, write the number on the chalkboard. Have students see how close they came to the correct number. Who had estimated more kernels than there were? Who had estimated fewer?

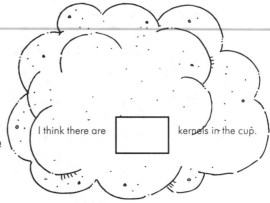

I think there are _____ kernels in the cup.

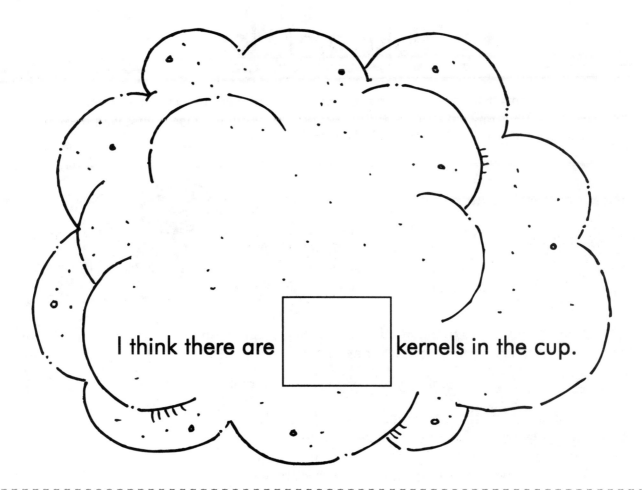

I think there are ☐ kernels in the cup.

I think there are ☐ kernels in the cup.

Real Math for Young Learners • EMC 744

Send a letter home asking parents to allow their child to help them cook something (page 31). Have children return their record sheets and explain to the class what was cooked and how they helped.

Measurement Center

Set up an exploration center containing measuring spoons, measuring cups, a kitchen scale, small plastic bowls, and a supply of rice and beans. Allow children to explore measuring into the bowls and weighing things on the scale.

After everyone has had an opportunity to explore measurement, discuss the discoveries they made. For example:

I found that it took four of these cups to make one of this cup.

I found out that a bowl of beans was heavier than a bowl of rice.

Set the Table

Provide a tablecloth, plastic dishes, glasses or cups, and flatware for this activity.

1. Spread the cloth over a table. Put stacks of dishes and flatware nearby. Set one place on the table. Select a child to set a second place just like yours at the other end of the table. Select two more children to set the sides of the table.

2. Place a stack of dishes, glasses, and flatware in the middle of an empty table. Say "Six people are going to eat at this table." Point to the dishes and ask "Do we have enough plates for six people? Do we have enough spoons (and so on)?" Have children place each dish or piece of flatware around the table to see if there are enough pieces. If there are not enough of an item, ask students to tell you how many more they need. If there are extras, ask students to tell you how many are left over.

3. Make this into a center activity. Put the tablecloth and dishes into a picnic basket or box. Make a set of cards showing various numbers of people coming to the picnic. Each child chooses a different card and puts out the required number of items.

Math at My House

Dear Parents,

Please allow your child to help you prepare part of a meal. Discuss how you are using counting and measurement as you cook. Have your child draw, write, or dictate while you fill in the record form at the bottom of this page.

Thank you for your help.

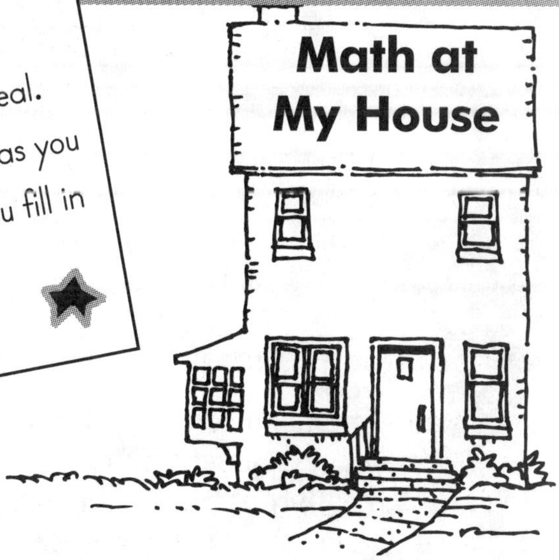

We cooked _____ at my house.

name of recipe

This is how I helped.

My name is _____ .

Read **The Doorbell Rang** by Pat Hutchins (Scholastic, 1986). Act out the story using a set of paper cookies (page 33). Then create your own problems following the suggestions below.

1. Use the set of paper cookies. Call up two children. Show two cookies and ask "Do we have enough cookies for _(children's names)_?" Hand one cookie to each child to verify that you do have enough. (If your students are ready for a more complicated concept, explain that each child has "half" of the cookies.)

2. Hold up four cookies. Ask "How many cookies can each person have?" Pass the cookies out one at a time. Ask "How many cookies did they each get?"

3. Call up another child. Hold up the four cookies again and ask "Do we have enough cookies for everyone?" Pass the cookies out. Ask "Did we have enough cookies?" and "How many did we have left over?"

4. Call up another child. Ask "How many cookies do I need so each person can have one?" Have someone come up and pass out one cookie to each child. Have the class help count the cookies as they are passed out. Make this more difficult by asking how many would be needed to give two or three cookies to each child.

5. End the activity by asking "How many cookies do I need to have if everyone in our class gets one cookie?" Record their responses, then pass out real cookies as the class counts to see if they were correct. (Don't forget the teacher!)

Reproduce the form on page 34 for children to do as they are enjoying their cookies.

Note: Reproduce the cookies to use with the activity on page 32.

 Real Math for Young Learners • EMC 744

My name is _____ .

Share the Cookies

Here are 6 cookies.
Share the cookies.

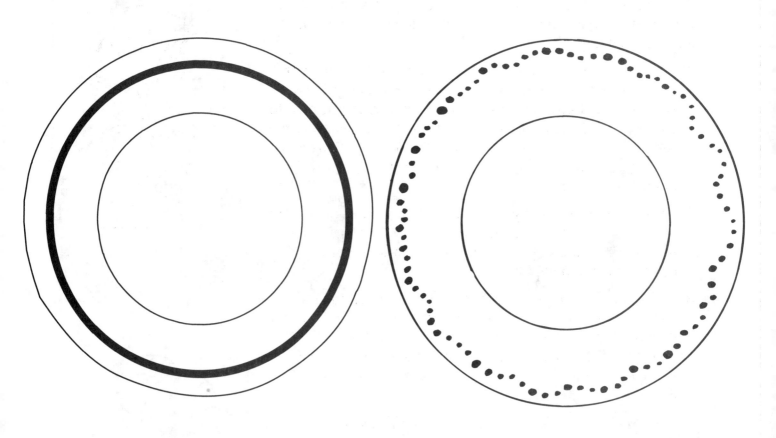

1. Color.

2. Cut.

3. Paste.

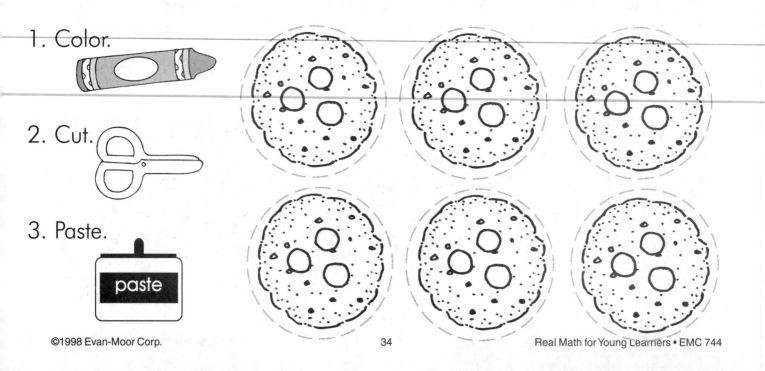

One Half, One Fourth

Reproduce two copies of the sandwich and pizza on page 36 for everyone doing the lesson. Have students color and cut out one set of pictures.

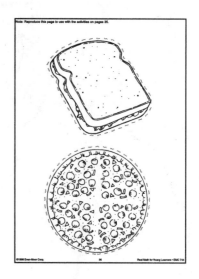

1. First work with the sandwich. Say "You have one sandwich. Your friend doesn't have any sandwich. How can you cut the sandwich to share with your friend? How can you be sure the pieces are the same size?" Have children show you how they would cut their sandwiches. Each time the cut is close to a half, hold up the two pieces and say " _(child's name)_ cut his/her sandwich in half."

2. After showing different ways to fold and cut the sandwich in half, give each student a second sandwich to cut. Explain that when something is cut into two same-size pieces , we call each piece one half.

3. Next, work with the pizza. Say "You have one pizza. Four people want to eat the pizza. How can you cut it so everyone gets a piece?" Have children show you how they would cut their pizzas. Each time the cut is close to fourths, hold up the four pieces and say " _(child's name)_ cut his/her pizza in fourths."

4. Take a pizza and show how to fold it in half and in half again to make even pieces. Explain that when something is cut into four same-size pieces , we call each piece one fourth. Give each student a second pizza to cut in the manner you demonstrated.

Note: Reproduce this page to use with the activities on page 35.

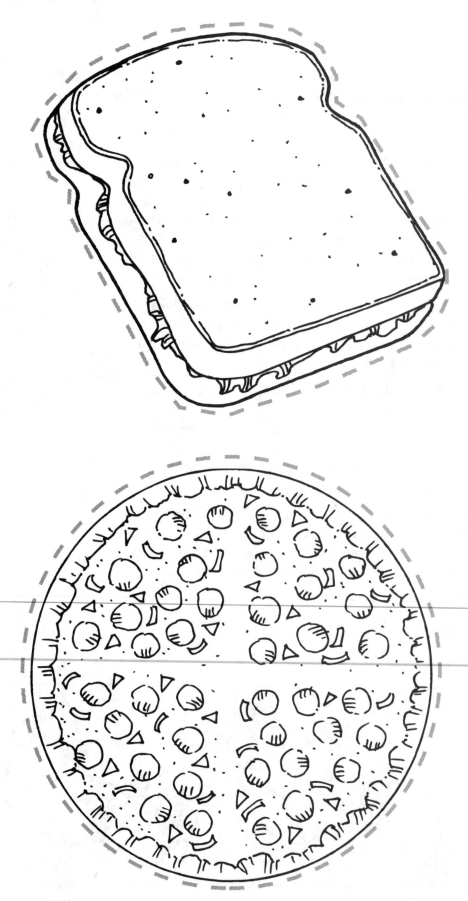

36

 # Math in the Bathroom

Discuss what you find in a bathroom (toilet, tub, sink, shower, medicine cabinet, towels, soap, etc.). Ask "What do we do in a bathroom?" If you get a limited number of ideas, ask questions to get the discussion started (brush teeth, take a bath, comb hair, etc.)

Tub or Shower?

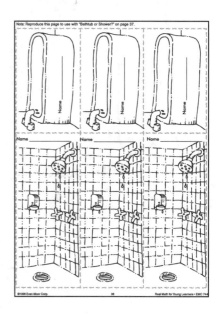

Reproduce a number of copies of the tub and shower pictures on page 38. Have each child take the picture that shows how he/she bathes at home. They are to write their name on the picture they choose and place it in the correct column on a graph titled "Do You Use a Tub or a Shower?" Some children will respond "I use both at my house." Either have children name the one they use most often, or add a "both" column to your graph.

Use the graph for counting practice and to answer questions such as:

> "How many people use tubs? showers?"
> "Did more people use tubs or showers?"
> "How many more?"

Bath Math

Use your water table and rubber toy ducks to practice beginning computation.

> "Put 3 ducks in the water. Now put in 2 more ducks. Who can tell us how many ducks are in the tub now? That's right—3 ducks and 2 ducks makes 5 ducks."

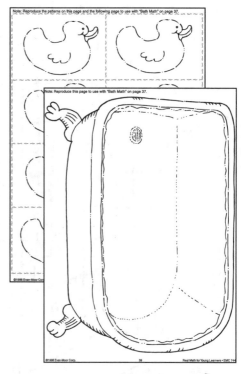

When students have done problems with "real" ducks, use the tub and duck patterns on pages 39 and 40. Work first as a class, using an overhead transparency of the tub. Then give every student a tub and ducks. Have them manipulate ducks as you give oral word problems.

If your students are ready, give them problems using symbols as well. Post the tub picture. Have a student put several ducks in the tub. Write the number on the chalkboard. Have a second student put more ducks in the tub. Write the numeral. Add the addition and equals signs to make an equation. Ask a third student to count how many ducks there are in all. Write the answer and read the equation with your students. Repeat the process with varying numbers of ducks.

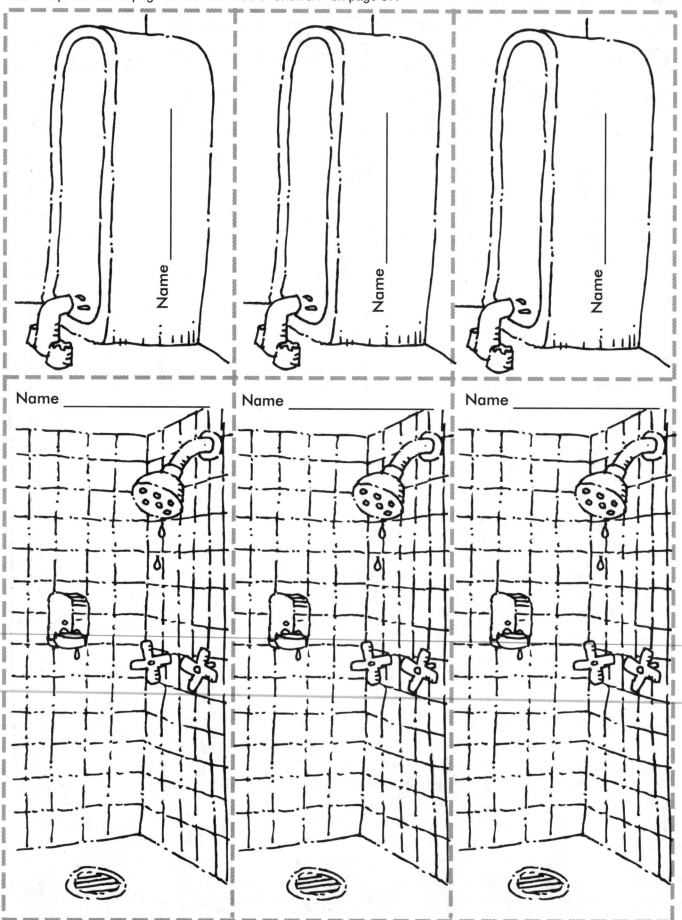

Name _____

Name _____

Name _____

Name

Name

Name

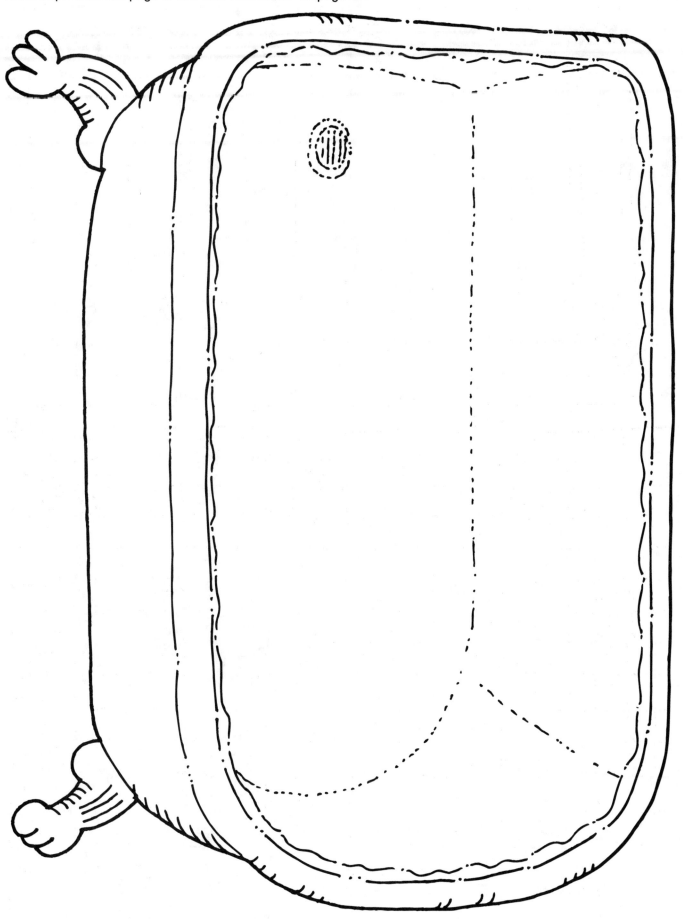

Note: Reproduce the patterns on this page to use with "Bath Math" on page 37.

40

Brush Those Teeth

Patterning with Your Toothbrush

Reproduce the toothbrush and toothpaste tube patterns on pages 42 and 43 on various colors of construction paper to use for patterning practice. Begin with simple ABAB patterns, moving on to more complicated ones when your students are ready. Vary the activity by having students copy a pattern, complete a pattern, and create patterns of their own.

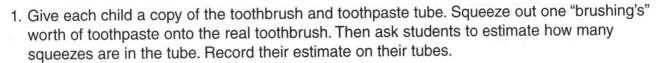

How Many Brushes in a Tube of Toothpaste?

Be sure students understand this is an "at school only" activity since it uses up a whole tube of toothpaste.

You will need:
- a toothbrush
- a full tube of toothpaste
- copies of the toothpaste tube (page 43)
- copies of the toothbrush (page 42)

1. Give each child a copy of the toothbrush and toothpaste tube. Squeeze out one "brushing's" worth of toothpaste onto the real toothbrush. Then ask students to estimate how many squeezes are in the tube. Record their estimate on their tubes.

2. Call one student at a time to bring his/her paper toothbrush. You hold the toothbrush as the student squeezes ONLY ONE brush's worth of toothpaste onto the brush. (Have extra tooth-brush patterns on hand in case some students get two turns to squeeze the tube.) When the tube is empty, count the toothbrushes to see how many squeezes were in the tube.

3. Have each student read the number on his/her toothpaste tube to see who came the closest.

4. Repeat the process with a second brand of the same size or the same brand in a different size to see how many "brushes" are in that tube.

"I Brushed My Teeth" Chart

Reproduce the toothbrushing chart on page 44. Send the forms home on a Monday to be returned the next Monday. Children mark each time they brush their teeth for one week.

Make a graph of the results when the forms are returned. Use the graph to ask questions requiring children to count and make comparisons.

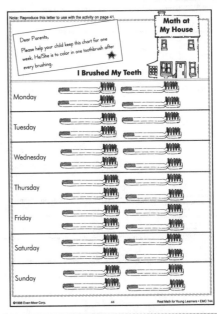

Note: Reproduce these patterns to use with the activities on page 41.

Note: Reproduce these patterns to use with the activities on page 41.

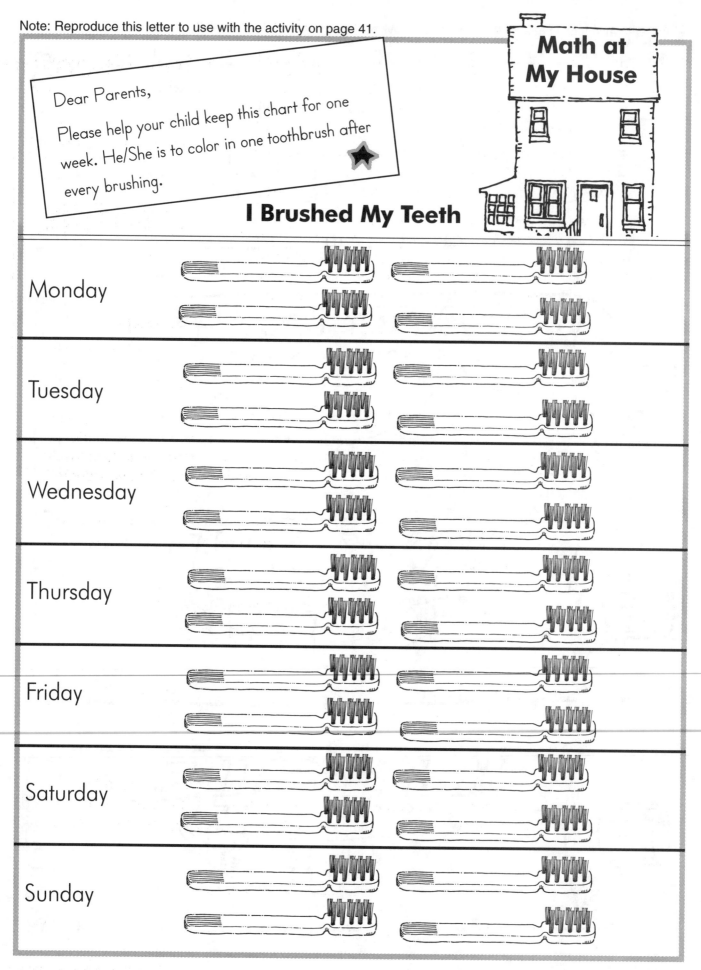

Math at My House

Dear Parents,

Please help your child keep this chart for one week. He/She is to color in one toothbrush after every brushing.

I Brushed My Teeth

Monday		
Tuesday		
Wednesday		
Thursday		
Friday		
Saturday		
Sunday		

 # Math in the Bedroom

How Many Beds in Your Bedroom?

Tell students to close their eyes and try to picture their own bedrooms. Ask "How many beds are in your bedroom? Do you have a big bed, a small bed, twin beds, or bunk beds?"

Make a "yes - no" picture graph showing the answer to the question "Do you have more than one bed in your bedroom?" Reproduce the bed patterns on page 46. Give one to each student. Have students write their names on their beds and place in the appropriate column. Count the beds in each column, then ask "Do more children have one bed or more than one bed in their bedroom?" "How many more?"

Count Your Bedroom

Talk about the types of things that are found in bedrooms (furniture, doors, light switches). Explain to students they will be counting these things in their own bedrooms. To model the activity, enlarge the pictures on page 47 and glue them to a chart set up to look like the record sheet. Have students count the number of each item found in the classroom. Record the numbers on the chart.

Reproduce page 47 as a homework assignment. When the forms are returned, have students compare their findings. Use the pictures on page 47 to make a Count Your Bedroom chart like the one shown here:

Count Your Bedroom						
🛏	0 0	1 5	2 8	3 0	4 0	5 0
🪑	0 4	1 6	2 3	3 0	4 0	5 0
🗄	0 11	1 4	2 1	3 0	4 0	5 0
🗄	0 0	1 8	2 7	3 0	4 0	5 0

Point to one object and say, "Everyone that has 0 (name object) stand up." Have the class count how many people are standing and write that number in the 0 box on the chart. Repeat for each number on the chart. When the row is complete, ask questions such as:

"Did anyone count 0? 1? 2? etc."
"How many people counted 4 (name object) in their house?"
"How many more people counted 2 than 4?"

Follow this procedure for all of the items on the chart.

Note: Reproduce these patterns to use with "How Many Beds..." on page 45.

Real Math for Young Learners • EMC 744

Note: Reproduce this form to use with "Count Your Bedroom" on page 45.

★ In _____'s Bedroom ★

How many do you see?

Explain to students that they are going to measure some real things using their own feet. Demonstrate how to walk heel-to-toe as you count the length of an object in the classroom (door or table for example). Have one or more students measure the same distance with their own feet. Ask "Why did it take more of _____'s feet than mine?"

Lay down a jump rope and provide time for each student to practice walking toe-to-heel and counting. An aide, volunteer, or cross-age tutor can supervise this activity.

Explain the record form (page 49) students will be taking home.

When the forms are returned, compare the results by arranging the sheets to form a graph. You will need a large floor area and labels for each column.

Have everyone hold their record sheet. Tell students to stand up when you say the number they have on their form. Start saying numbers by "feet" beginning with one "foot." When the first students stand up, have them bring their papers to form the first column of the graph. Lay out the forms. Label this column with a card telling the number of "feet." Continue with "feet" measurements, laying out the forms, until all papers have been collected. Use this giant graph to make comparisons. Ask questions such as "How many children have a bed five 'feet' long?" "Which length did most children have?" or "How many children had a bed longer than yours? shorter than yours? the same size as yours?" Discuss why there were differences in measurment.

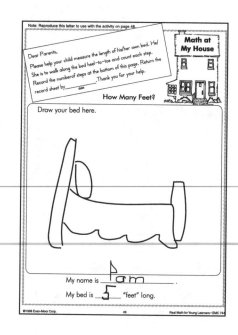

Math at My House

Dear Parents,

Please help your child measure the length of his/her own bed. He/She is to walk along the bed heel-to-toe and count each step. Record the number of steps at the bottom of this page. Return the record sheet by _____ .Thank you for your help.
date

How Many Feet?

Draw your bed here.

My name is _____ .

My bed is _____ "feet" long.

Real Math for Young Learners • EMC 744

1. Use the verse to practice the number words one to ten.

   Make a transparency of "Ten in Bed" (page 51). Box the number words with a bright color. Make a set of cards containing the same number words.

   Teach the pattern of the verse to your students. As they recite the verse, point to the number word to emphasize it. Pass out the word cards and have each child come up to the chart to match his/her number word.

2. Practice the concept of subtraction by dramatizing it. Tape a "bed" area on your classroom floor. Select 10 children to "sleep" on the bed. Write the numeral 10 on the chalkboard to show how many children are in bed.

   Have children recite or sing the first verse. At the end of the verse, have the first child roll out of bed. Write the number 1 to show how many went away. Have the class count the number of children still in the bed. Write the numeral 9 on the chalkboard. Add a - and = sign to create a number sentence. Show your students how to read the equation. Repeat with each stanza of the verse.

Ten in Bed

There were ten in bed,

And the little one said,

Roll over, roll over.

So they all rolled over,

And one fell out.

There were nine in bed,
(Repeat rest of the first stanza.)
There were eight in bed...
There were seven in bed...
There were six in bed...
There were five in bed...
There were four in bed...
There were two in bed...

There was one in bed,

And the little one said,

I've got the whole mattress to myself!

(Ho-hum. I think I'll go to sleep!)

Math and Your Clothes

Developing Clothing Vocabulary

Begin by naming the articles of clothing that your students are wearing. To eliminate the "underwear giggles," deal only with clothes that you can see. Make sure students can identify shirts, pants, socks, shoes, hats, jackets, coats, vests, neckties, skirts, and dresses. Add describing words that are helpful. Students should understand terms such as: stripes, plaid, ruffle, collar, sleeve, zipper, buttons.

Check for Understanding

Have students stand to show whether they are wearing a specific article of clothing when you name it. Add descriptors until only one student is standing.

For example:

Stand up if you have a shirt on.

Keep standing if your shirt has a collar.

Keep standing if your shirt has a pocket.

Keep standing if your shirt has buttons.

Keep standing if your shirt is striped.

Keep standing if your shirt has red in it.

A Clothing Survey

1. Reproduce the stand-up clothes labels on pages 53 and 54. Put a small plastic glass by each stand up tag.

2. Have a student stand up. Analyze that student's clothes.

   Put a counter (a bean works well) into the glass by each tag that names an article of clothing the student is wearing. Do the same for each student in the class. (After the initial demonstration, you may want to complete this as a small group or individual activity conducted by a parent or cross-age helper.)

3. When all students have had their clothing analyzed, look at the glasses. Help your students to interpret this "graph" by asking questions such as:

   • Which glass is the fullest? What does that mean?

   • Which glass is the emptiest? What does that mean?

4. Count the counters in each glass with the class. Write the results on the glasses. Ask more questions to encourage analysis of the project.

   • Which has more, skirts or pants? How many more?

   • Which has less, socks or hats? How many less?

Note: Reproduce this page to use with "A Clothing Survey" on page 52.

fold

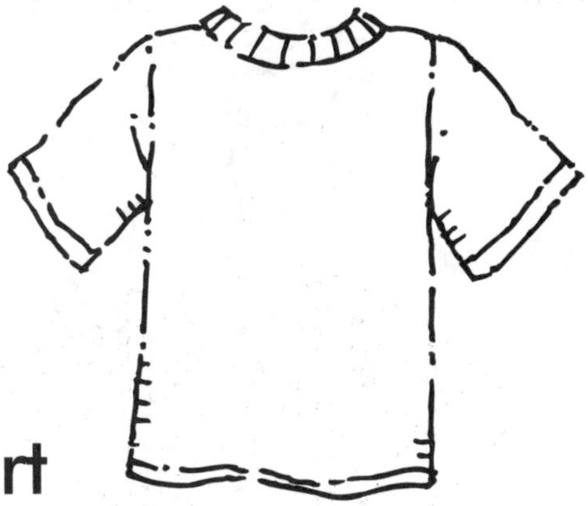

shirt

fold

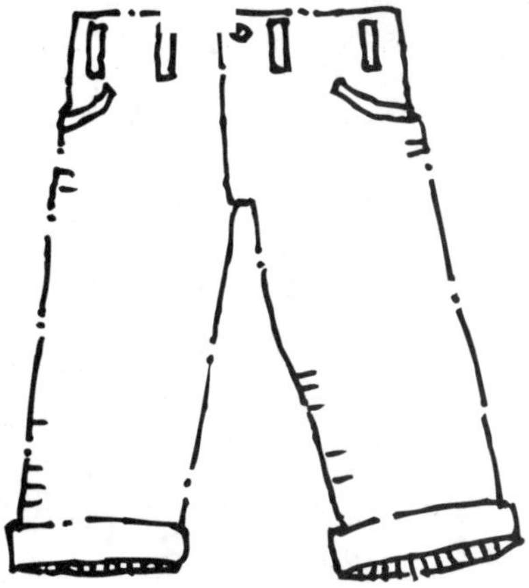

pants

fold

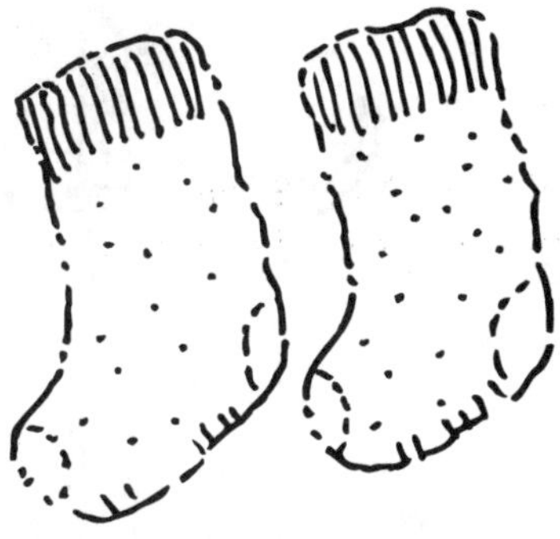

socks

fold

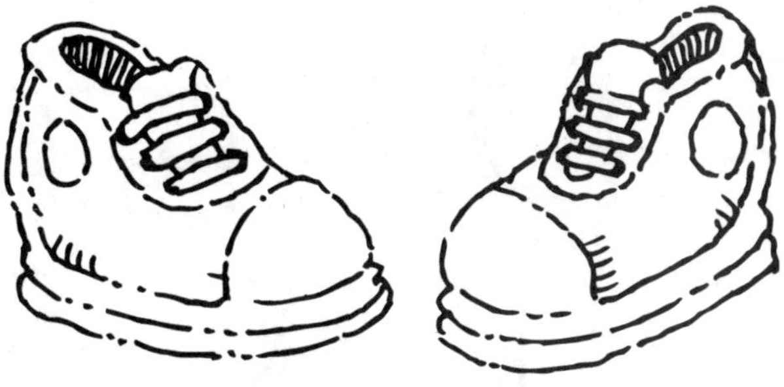

shoes

Note: Reproduce this page to use with "A Clothing Survey" on page 52.

fold

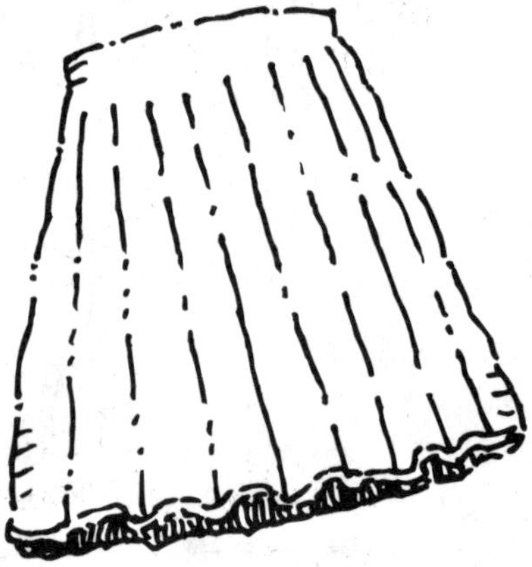

skirt

fold

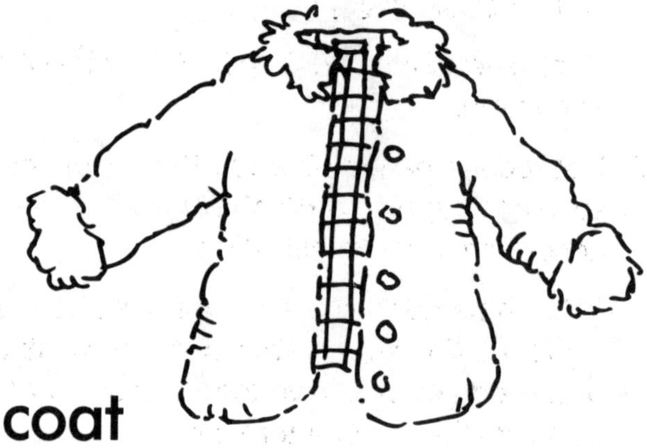

coat

fold

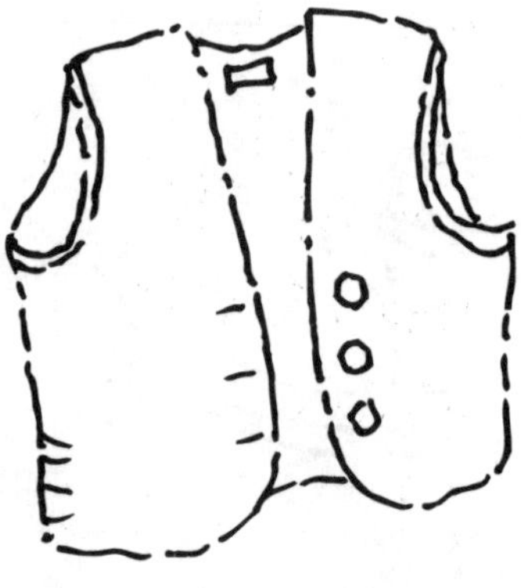

vest

fold

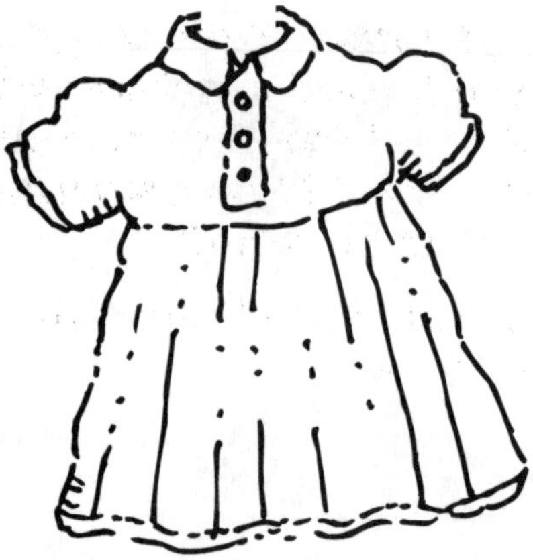

dress

Shirts, Shirts, Shirts

Sorting

1. Sort the shirts in your classroom by having students stand in groups representing the type of shirt that they are wearing.

   (For example: All shirts with buttons stand here. All shirts without buttons stand here.) Begin with two simple classifications.

   Sort several times using different classifications each time.

2. Reproduce pages 57 and 58 for each student. Have students cut the shirts apart and sort them according to a classification.

   ("Put the striped shirts in one pile and the shirts without stripes in another pile.") After students have practiced sorting, have them sort according to a classification they determine.

   As you check their work, they should be able to tell you their sorting "rule" and which of their groups is larger.

Note: Shirts can be sorted using any combination of these attributes: white/striped/plaid; collar/no collar; short sleeves/long sleeves; buttons/no buttons; pocket/no pocket.

Comparing the Groups

Reproduce pages 57 and 58 for this activity.

Have students compare the groups by placing each classification in a row. Now the interpretation can be more exact. "How many more striped shirts than plain shirts are there? How many more button shirts than collar shirts are there?"

Encourage students to sort the shirts in several different ways.

I PUT THE STRIPED SHIRTS WITH COLLARS IN THIS PILE AND THE STRIPED SHIRTS WITHOUT COLLARS IN THAT PILE.

THERE ARE 3 MORE PLAIN SHIRTS THAN STRIPED SHIRTS.

Patterning with Shirts

Have students pattern with the shirts on page 57 and 58. Begin by starting a pattern: checked shirt, white shirt, checked shirt, white shirt. Ask students to tell what should come next. Increase the complexity of the patterns as appropriate for your class.

• Have students create their own patterns and read them aloud.

• Give students a type of pattern (example: ABCABC) and have them create a shirt pattern that matches the type (checked, white, striped; checked, white, striped)

• Challenge students to create a single row of shirts that has several patterns.

Show Me with Shirts

Duplicate and cut out the football jerseys on pages 59 and 60. Each student will need the jerseys numbered 0-9.

Ask specific math questions appropriate to the ability of your class and have students respond by holding up the appropriate shirt.

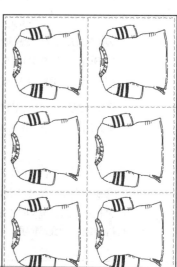

• Show me a 2.

• What is 4 + 3?

• What is one more than 5?

• Show me one more than 4.

• Show me 2 + 1 + 3.

Have students place the shirts in numerical order.

Ordinal Numbers

Reproduce page 61 for each student. Give oral directions using ordinal numbers.

• Put your finger on the third shirt in the first row.

• Color the first shirt in the second row red.

• Draw a pocket on the second shirt in the second row.

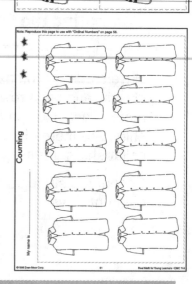

Note: Reproduce this page to use with the activities on pages 55 and 56.

Note: Reproduce this page to use with the activities on pages 55 and 56.

Note: Reproduce this page to use with "Show Me with Shirts" on page 56.

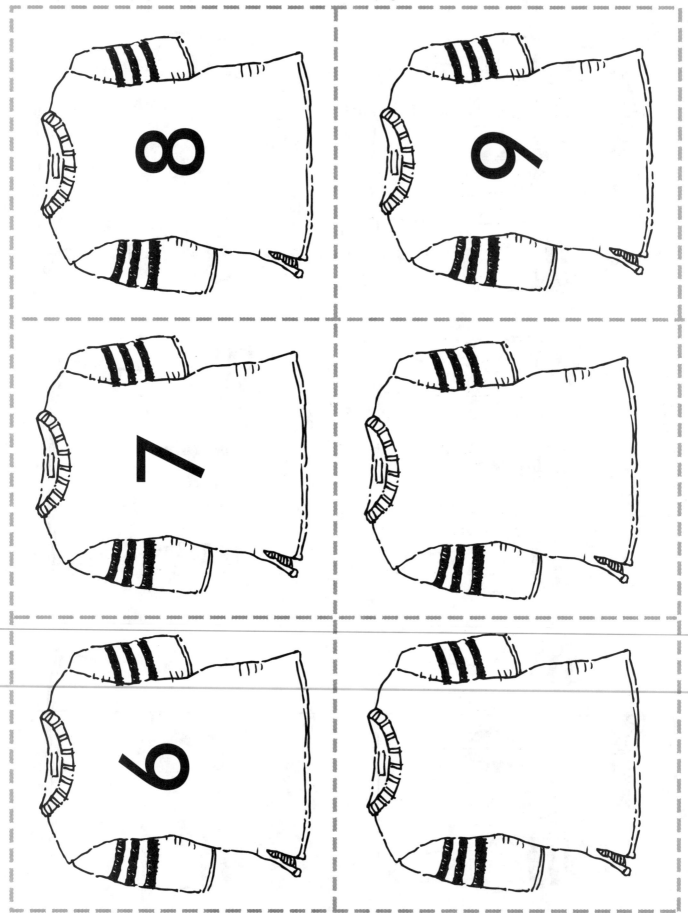

Counting

My name is _____

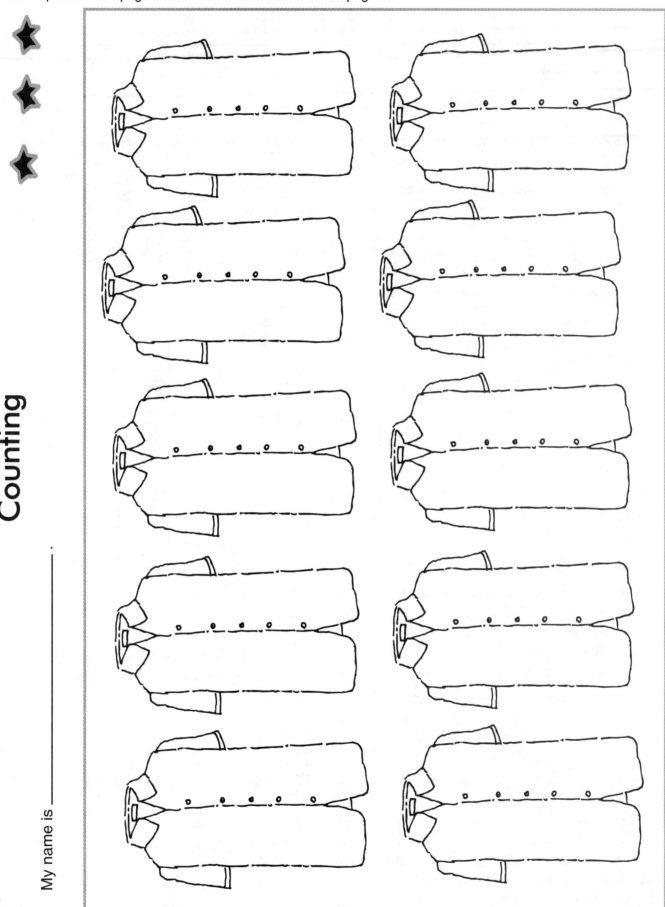

A Pair of Pants

Sorting Pants

1. Sort the students in your class by the type of pants that they are wearing. Have them stand in lines to make a real graph comparing the different types of pant. (Students in skirts or dresses could hold the line labels or form a no-pants category.)

   Record students' observations about the results of this real pants graph. (example: More people have long pants than short pants.)

2. Reproduce the pants patterns on pages 63 and 64. Have students sort the patterns into different groups. Be sure that students can explain their "rules for sorting."

Note: Pants can be sorted using any combination of these attributes: long/short; pocket/no pocket; zippers/buttons/cuffs; flowers/plaid/plain.

Pockets in Pants

Have students count the pockets in their pants. Tally the results of the count. Analyze the results of your tally.

Matching Pants to Legs

Reproduce page 65 for each student. Before students complete the worksheet, discuss the difficulties a tailor would have if making pants for animals with more than two legs.

Counting by Twos

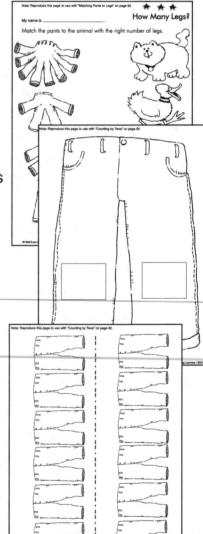

1. Reproduce the large pants pattern on page 66 to make ten pairs of pants. Put the pants on the wall or the chalkboard. Count the pants legs. Count again and write the numbers on the legs as you count them. (The even number should always be on the right leg.)

    Explain to students that there is a shortcut to counting called counting by twos. Circle the numeral on the right leg of each pair of pants. Now count by twos, calling out the circled numerals only.

2. Reproduce page 67. Cut one row of pants for each student. Count the legs out loud as a class. Count the legs again as students write the numerals on the legs. Finally count the legs a third time as students circle the even numbers on the right legs. At this point, students count by twos, reading the circled numbers only.

Note: Reproduce this page to use with the sorting activity on page 62.

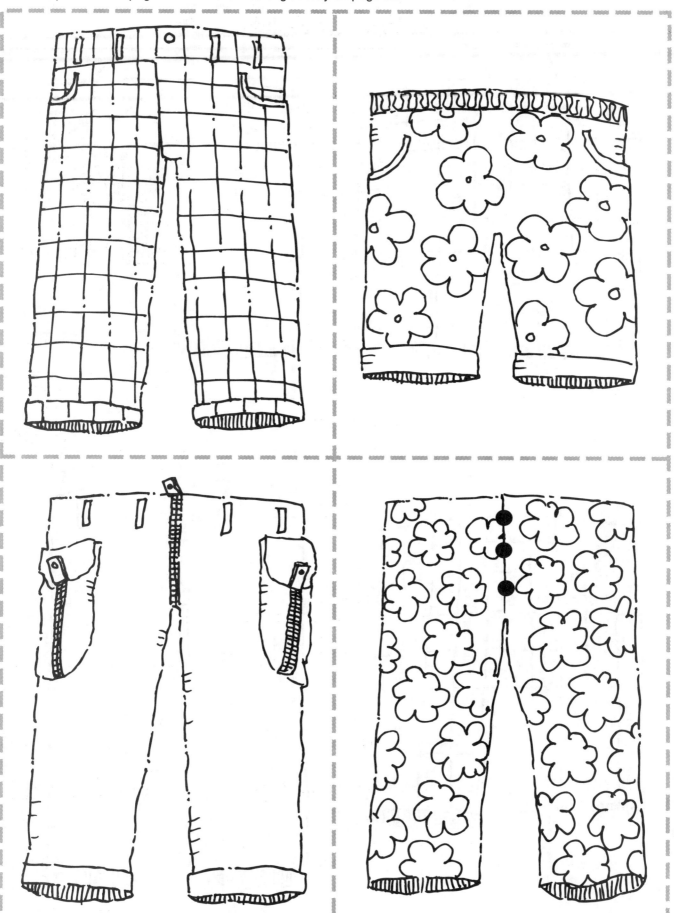

Note: Reproduce this page to use with the sorting activity on page 62.

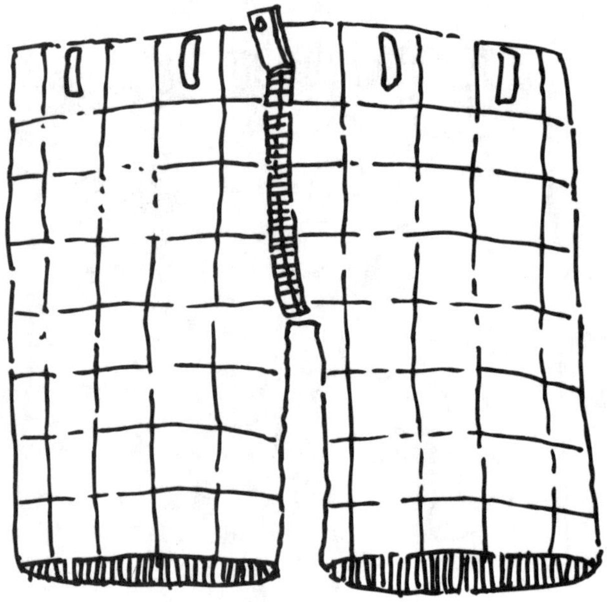

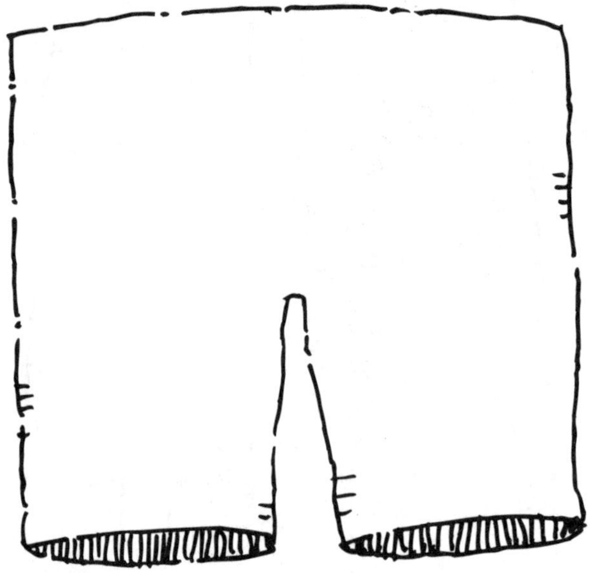

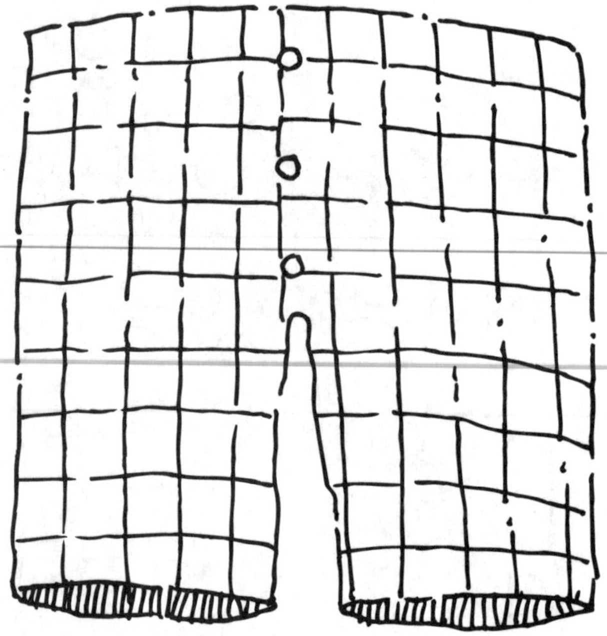

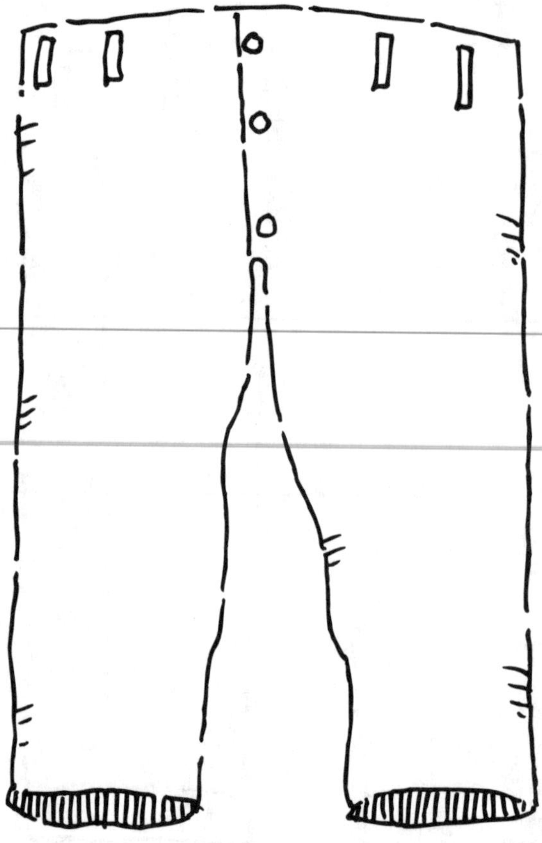

Note: Reproduce this page to use with "Matching Pants to Legs" on page 62.

How Many Legs?

My name is _____ .

Match the pants to the animal with the right number of legs.

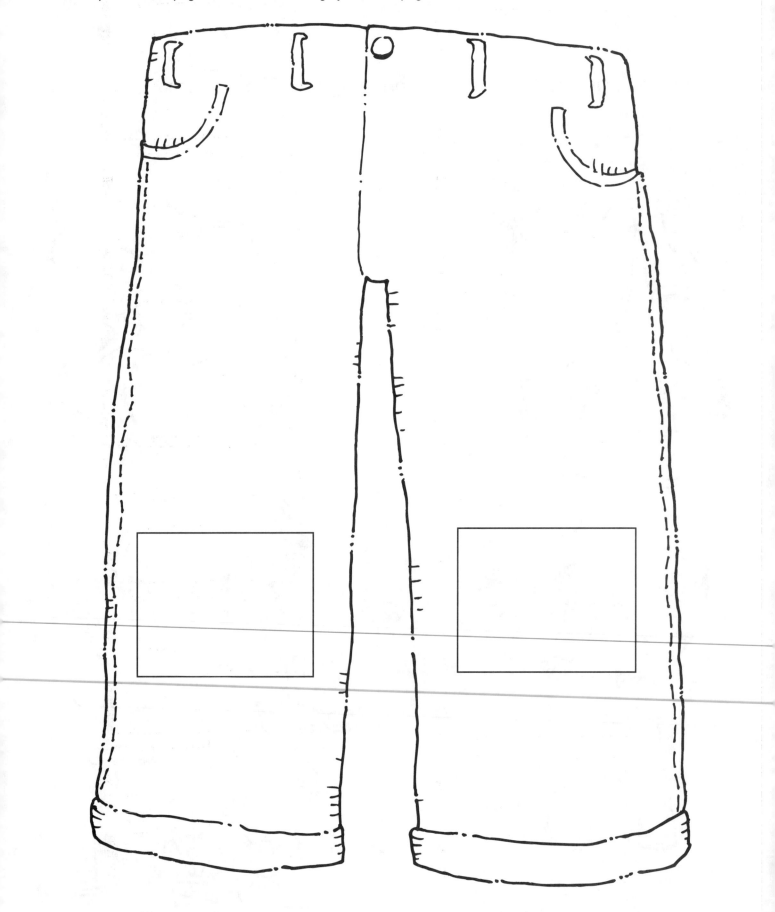

Note: Reproduce this page to use with "Counting by Twos" on page 62.

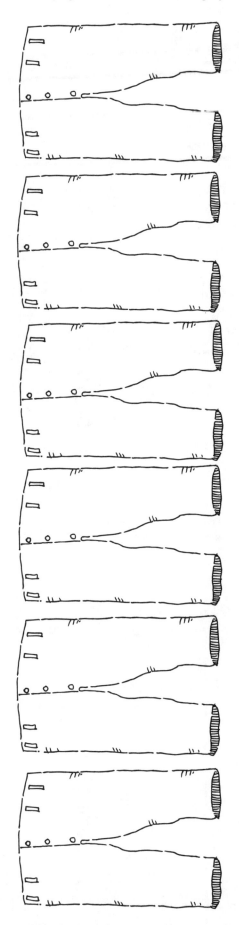

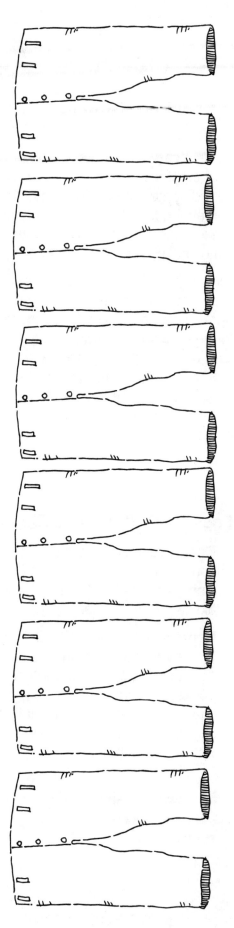

Coats

A Coat Rack Graph

Lay all the items found on your coat rack (coats, hats, mittens, boots, scarves, sweaters, backpacks, etc.) out on the floor. Sort the items on the floor grid. When the graph is complete, spend some time discussing it. Ask students to tell you something they know after looking at the graph. Accept any reasonable answer. Then question the group to elicit any conclusions that they might have overlooked.

Explain that you would like a record of the graph, but that you understand that the students will need to take their coats and backpacks home. Ask for suggestions. Your class may decide to create a picture graph. They would draw pictures of each item of clothing and then use the illustrations on the grid. Or they might decide to make a symbolic graph. They might put their names by each type of item that they are wearing. (If they have more than one item in a category they should put up their names twice.)

Pockets, Buttons, and Zippers

1. Choose one coat from your coat rack or use your own coat. Count the buttons, pockets, and zippers on the coat. Keep track by stacking blocks or making tally marks.

2. Reproduce the Coat Check Record on page 70. Show how to record the results of your count on the page. Students then count the pockets, zippers, and buttons on their own coats and record their results on an individual coat check record. (Recording can be done with a parent helper.)

3. Use the coat check record pages as the basis for new comparisons, for example: Who has the most pockets? How many have only one zipper?, etc.

My Coat

I have _____ buttons on my coat.

I have _____ zippers on my coat.

I have _____ pockets on my coat.

Looking at Coats

Talk with your class about what makes coats different. (Sue's coat is red and Tom's coat is blue. Tim has a zipper and Sam has buttons.)

Use Venn Diagrams to group the coats. Make two overlapping circles on the floor with yarn. Label each circle with a word that could describe a coat (red, furry, zippered, slick, black, waterproof, etc.). Have students place their coats in the circle or circles that match their coats. Coats that match both characteristics would go in the overlapping area. Coats that do not match either characteristic would go outside the two circles.

Change labels and repeat the activity.

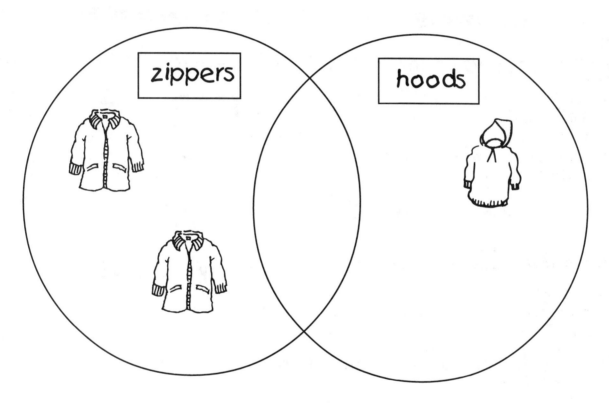

One-to-One Correspondence

Reproduce page 71 for each student. Have students cut out the coats and glue them to the hooks.

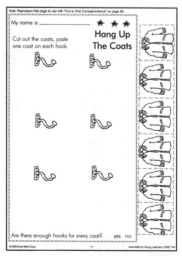

Note: Reproduce this page to use with "Pockets, Buttons, and Zippers" on page 68.

My Coat

I have _____ buttons on my coat.

I have _____ zippers on my coat.

I have _____ pockets on my coat.

My Coat

I have _____ buttons on my coat.

I have _____ zippers on my coat.

I have _____ pockets on my coat.

My Coat

I have _____ buttons on my coat.

I have _____ zippers on my coat.

I have _____ pockets on my coat.

My Coat

I have _____ buttons on my coat.

I have _____ zippers on my coat.

I have _____ pockets on my coat.

     Real Math for Young Learners • EMC 744

My name is _____ .

Cut out the coats, paste
one coat on each hook.

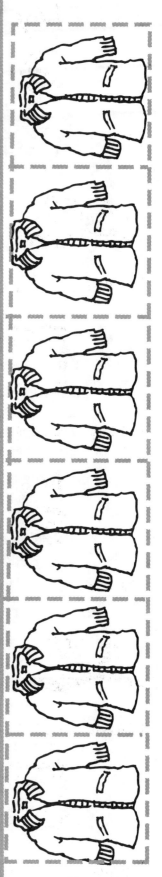

Are there enough hooks for every coat?   yes   no

Hats, Hats, Hats

Literature Connection

Read **Caps for Sale** by Esphyr Slobodkina. Discuss the pattern of the caps that the peddler wears. Provide real caps and act out the story. (The caps do not have to match those described in the story; young imaginations make up for differences.)

Reproduce the activity sheet on page 74. Students cut out the peddler and his hats and glue them onto a 6" x 18" (15 x 45.5 cm) piece of paper. Color the hats to create a new pattern for the peddler. Allow time for students to show and read their new patterns to other members of the class.

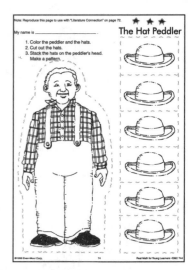

Following Directions

Reproduce the activity page on page 75. Have students follow oral directions to complete the page. Vary the complexity of the oral directions to met your students' needs.

For example:

1. Draw two blue hats on the cat's head. Draw one red hat on top. How many hats are on the cat? If the class is working with symbols, write the number on the line in the sentence.

2. Draw a black hat on the dog. Add a yellow hat and a green hat. How many hats are on the dog?

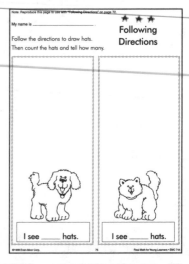

Adding On

1. Choose a student to be the "hat rack." Show simple addition problems by adding on. Start by putting two real hats on the "hat rack." Add one more hat. How many hats are on the rack? Continue to demonstrate with different number combinations. A recorder can write the number sentence demonstrated.

2. Reproduce page 76. Depending on skill level, give each student a number of paper hats. As you tell a story problem, students show it with their paper hats.

   Encourage students to tell their own adding-on problems.

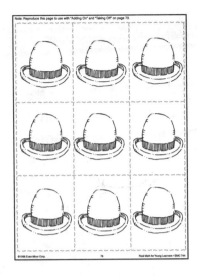

Taking Off

1. Reverse the procedure to demonstrate subtraction. Start again with your human hat rack and real hats. Put a number of hats on the rack. Take two hats off. How many hats are left?

2. After students are comfortable with the idea of taking off hats, have them demonstrate subtraction problems using the paper hats. Write the number sentences as the problems are demonstrated.

TWO HATS AND ONE MORE HAT MAKES THREE HATS.

Note: Reproduce this page to use with "Literature Connection" on page 72.

The Hat Peddler

My name is _____ .

1. Color the peddler and the hats.
2. Cut out the hats.
3. Stack the hats on the peddler's head.
   Make a pattern.

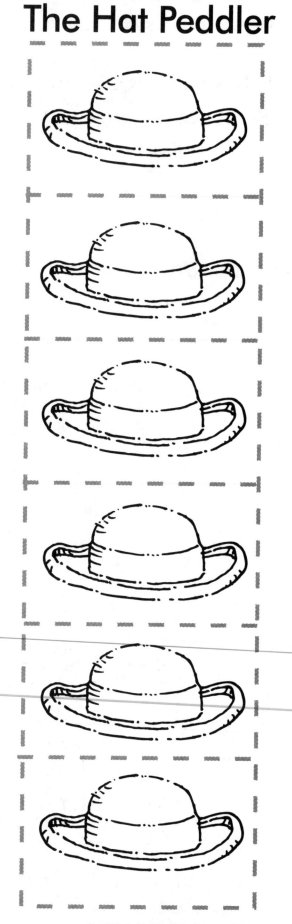

Real Math for Young Learners • EMC 744

My name is _____.

Follow the directions to draw hats.

Then count the hats and tell how many.

Following Directions

I see _____ hats.

I see _____ hats.

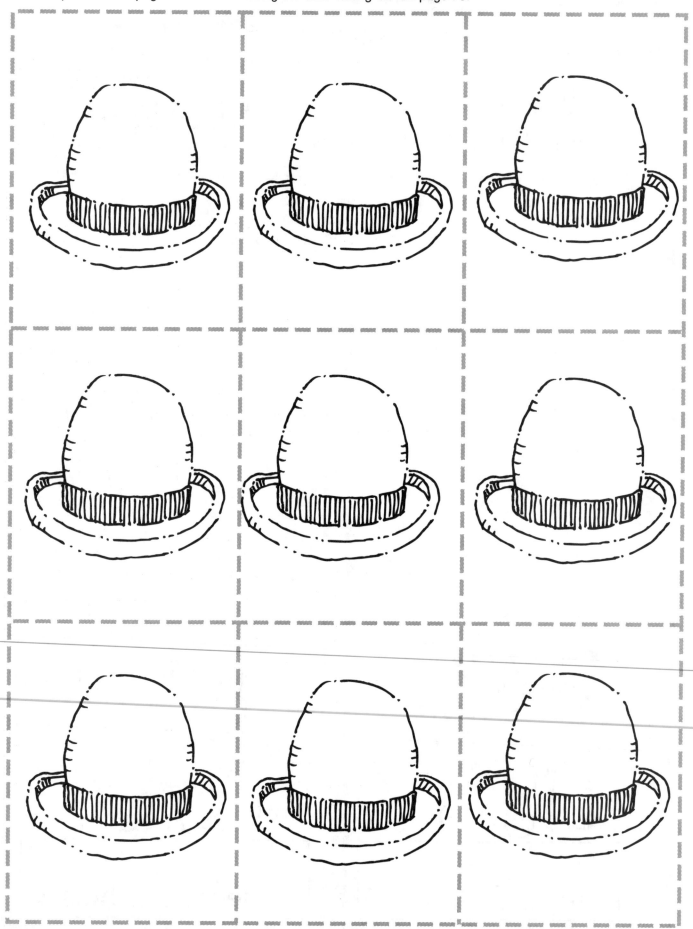

Neckties

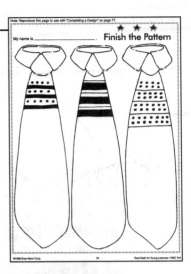

Completing a Design

1. Bring several real neckties to your classroom. Discuss the patterns on the neckties.

2. Reproduce the ties on page 78 for each student. The pattern has been started on each tie, but needs to be completed by the students. After they complete the pattern, have them color the ties so that the colors repeat just as the design does.

Longest to Shortest

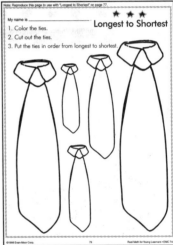

1. Cut several neckties out of felt or colored paper. Make them different lengths. Display the neckties and have students arrange them in order from longest to shortest.

2. Reproduce the activity page on page 79. Have students cut out the ties and arrange them in order of length. Point out that if one looks at the order from the other end of the row, the ties go from shortest to longest.

Necktie Symmetry

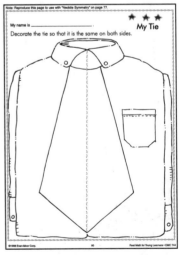

1. Draw a large tie on a piece of poster board. Divide the tie in half by drawing a line from the top to the bottom. Place tie on floor and seat children in a circle around it. Challenge the class to help you design the tie so that both sides are exactly the same.

2. Provide parquetry blocks or construction paper shapes to make the designs. Place a shape on one side of the tie and have a student place an identical shape on the other side of the tie in the same position. Continue alternating sides until a pleasing design is created.

   You may choose to introduce the term symmetrical at this point. Explain that the tie is symmetrical because it can be divided in half and the two halves are identical.

3. After you have conducted the symmetrical tie activity as a whole group, set it up in a center for two students to explore independently.

4. Reproduce page 80 for students to create a symmetrical tie of their own.

Note: Reproduce this page to use with "Completing a Design" on page 77.

My name is _____ .

Finish the Pattern

My name is _____.

Longest to Shortest

1. Color the ties.
2. Cut out the ties.
3. Put the ties in order from longest to shortest.

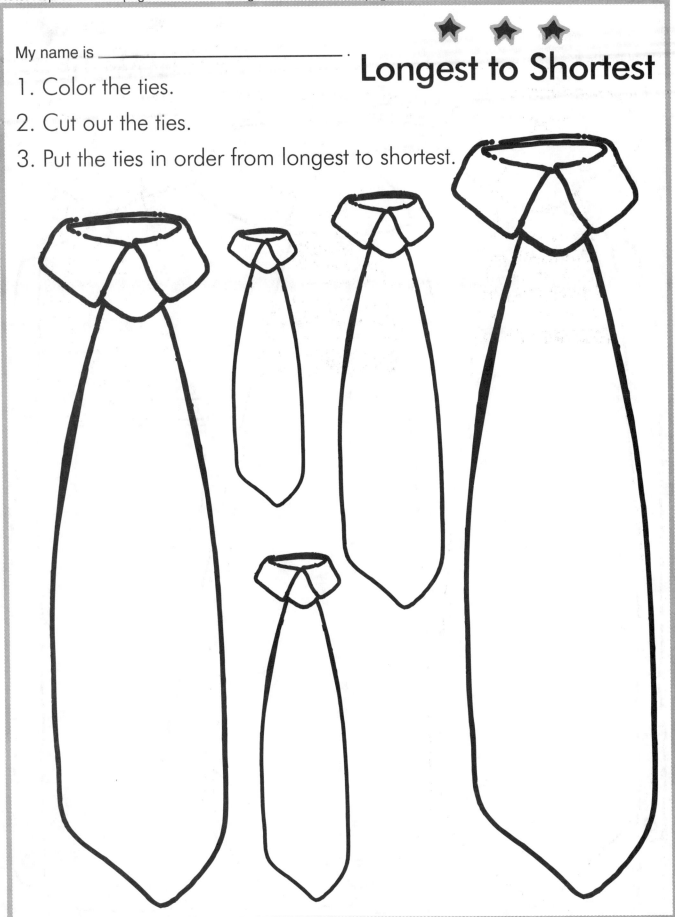

My name is _____ .

My Tie

Decorate the tie so that it is the same on both sides.

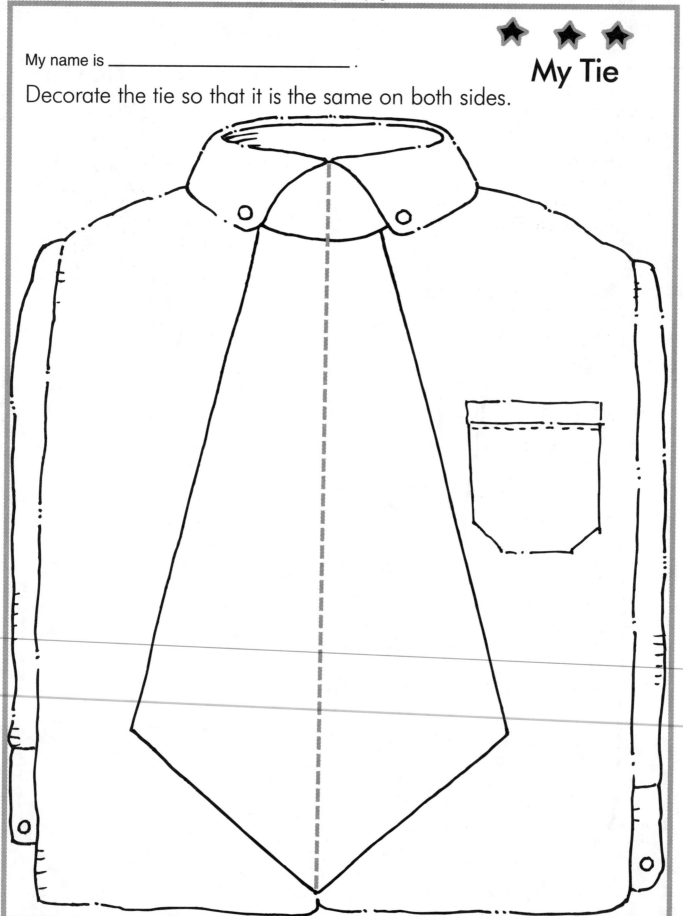

Belts

How Long Should It Be?

1. Choose a stuffed animal. Explain to your class that the animal needs a belt. Allow students to look at the animal.

2. Pass rolls of adding machine tape and scissors. Each child cuts a length of tape that he/she thinks will fit the animal.

3. Try the paper belts on the animal. Classify the estimates as too short, just right, and too long. Tape the belts up in their groups.

Note: This is another "graph." Ask students to interpret the results for you.

Decorate a Belt

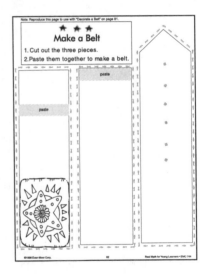

1. Reproduce the belt pattern on page 82. Have students cut and glue to make a belt.

2. Students then decorate the belt in a repeating pattern.

3. Challenge students to find someone the belt fits.

Measuring with Belts

Use the belts that students have decorated as nonstandard units for measuring. Have teams of students measure items in the classroom and report their results.
(Example: Mrs. Sparkman's desk is four belts long. The chalkboard is six belts long.)

Make a Belt

1. Cut out the three pieces.

2. Paste them together to make a belt.

paste

paste

Scarves

Literature Connection

Read *The Long Red Scarf* by Nette Hilton. Grandpa tries to find someone to knit him a big, long, fuzzy, red scarf. Reproduce page 85 and have students follow directions to color the scarves.

Identifying Geometric Shapes

Use shape blocks or shapes cut from paper to practice identifying those geometric shapes appropriate for your students.

Reproduce the scarf pattern on page 86.

Direct students to identify the geometric shapes on the scarf by coloring them.

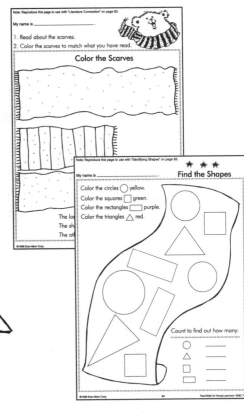

WHO CAN TELL ME THE NAME OF THIS SHAPE?

Making a Shape Scarf

Let students decorate their own "scarves."

Materials:
- rectangles of white paper (one per student)
- small paper plates for paint
- poster paint
- shapes to print

To make shapes for printing:

Cut sponges in circles, squares, rectangles, and triangles; or use the edges of a small milk carton (square), small box (rectangle), juice can (circle), and three rectangles of cardboard taped together (triangle).

Steps to Follow:

1. Dip the shape into a puddle of paint on a plate.

2. Press the shape down and lift. Do not rub the paper with the shape.

3. Continue printing to fill the scarf with shapes.

4. Let the paint dry.

Counting the Shapes

When the scarf squares are dry, have students count the number of prints of each shape that they used. Use this data to create graph. You can use the blank grid on page 87.

Graphing the Scarves

When the individual graphs are completed, use them to create a class summary graph.

1. Put out the floor grid.

2. Have all students who used more circles than any other shape put their individual graphs or their names in one column.

3. Have all students who used more triangles than any other shape put their graphs in a second column.

4. Continue for rectangles and squares.

5. Ask students to interpret this summary graph.

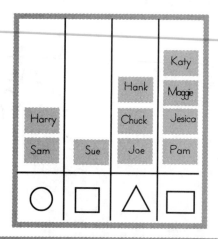

My name is _____.

1. Read about the scarves.

2. Color the scarves to match what you have read.

Color the Scarves

The longest scarf is red.

The shortest scarf is blue and red striped.

The other scarf is blue.

My name is _____ .

Find the Shapes

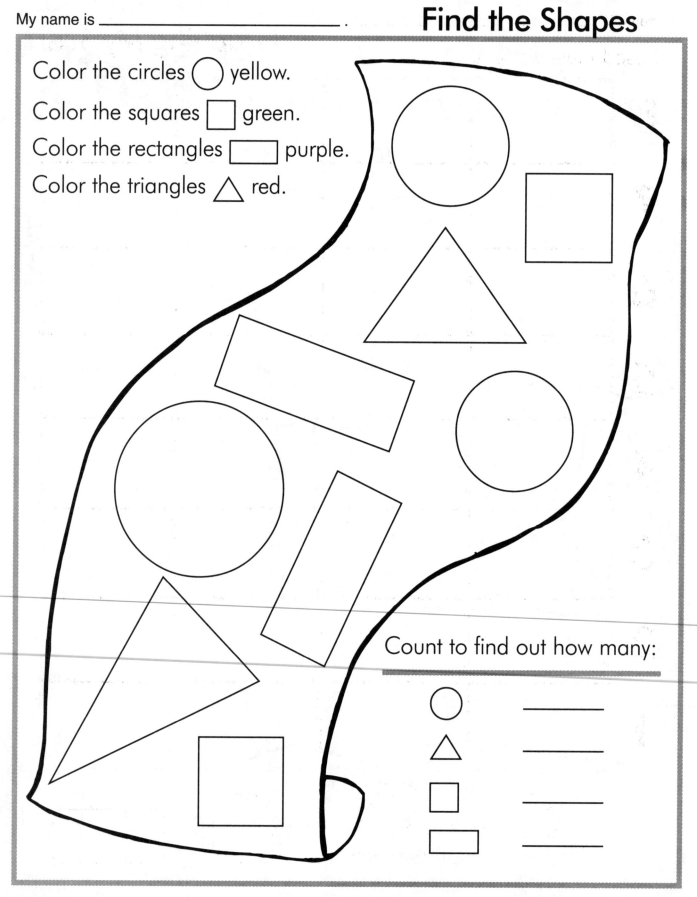

Color the circles ◯ yellow.

Color the squares ▢ green.

Color the rectangles ▭ purple.

Color the triangles △ red.

Count to find out how many:

◯ _____

△ _____

▢ _____

▭ _____

★ ★ ★

My name is _____ .

Graphing My Scarf

I used these shapes.

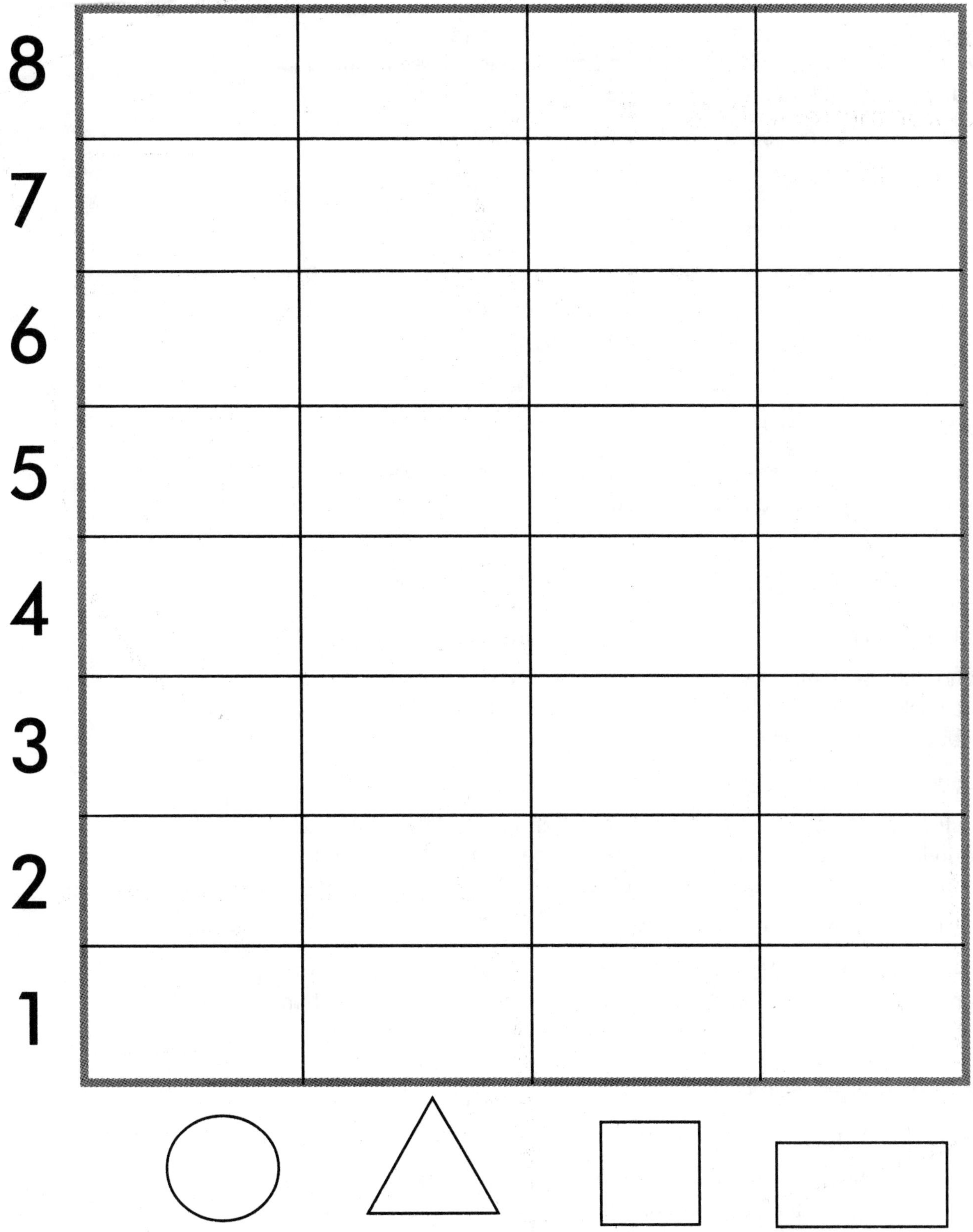

8				
7				
6				
5				
4				
3				
2				
1				

◯ △ ☐ ▭

Math Skills: sorting, number order, readiness for addition and subtraction, patterning

Shoes and Socks

Finding Pairs

Provide a tub of real socks for sorting. Separate pairs and mix the socks up. Have students work in small groups to find the pairs. The difficulty increases if you use socks that are nearly identical.

Help students to develop some strategies for finding the matches:

- Begin by sorting into colors.
- Check toes for special markings.
- Look at the length of the sock.

Reproduce page 90. Have students cut out the socks, match the pairs, and glue them to another piece of paper.

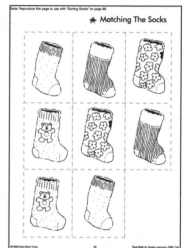

A Special Number Line

1. Suspend a length of clothesline or heavy twine across the front of your room. Be sure to make the line an appropriate height for your students.

2. Have students clothespin numbered socks in order to the clothesline. Use real ones that you have pinned numbers on or copy the sock patterns on page 91 and write numbers on them.

3. When students have practiced putting the numbers in order, leave the socks in place to use as a number line. Practice adding and subtracting on the line.

   An addition problem: $4 + 2 = ?$

   A student points to the sock numbered 4 and moves to the right counting two more socks. The student is now pointing at the sock numbered 6. The answer to the problem is 6.

   A subtraction problem: $8 - 5 = ?$

   A student points to the sock numbered 8 and moves to the left counting five socks. The student is now pointing at the sock numbered 3. The answer to the problem is 3.

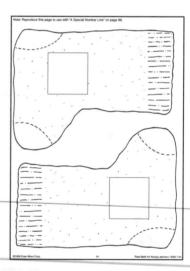

Patterning with Socks

Have students create a pattern using real socks.

 Note: Since you have been talking about pairs, it will help to have students sort and group the socks before beginning patterning. (Example: all striped socks, all dark toes, all plain socks)

Sorting Shoes

1. Have each student take off one shoe.

2. Practice sorting by grouping shoes that share attributes. Start with only two attributes and add more as your students are ready.

3. Model several attributes and then have the students suggest the attributes.

   "I see some high-top shoes and some low-top shoes."

   "Can you put them in piles?"

   "I see some tie shoes and some buckle shoes."

   "Can you put them in piles?"

   "Shaundra, can you suggest a name for a new pile?"

Matching Shoes

After sorting the shoes, use them for a matching exercise.

One student chooses a shoe from the pile and then matches that shoe to its mate on someone's foot.

Little—Big—Biggest

1. Reproduce the monster figures on page 95 on an overhead transparency.

   Use them to introduce the concept of little, big, biggest.

2. Reproduce the shoes on pages 92-94. Show one pair of each size—little, big, biggest.

3. Have students sort the shoes into three piles—little, big, biggest.

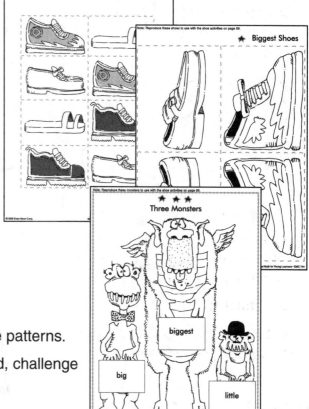

Patterning with Shoes

Use the shoes from pages 92-94 to make shoe patterns.

After using size as the attribute being patterned, challenge students to use other attributes.

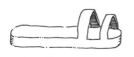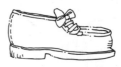

Note: Reproduce this page to use with "Finding Pairs" on page 88.

⭐ Matching The Socks

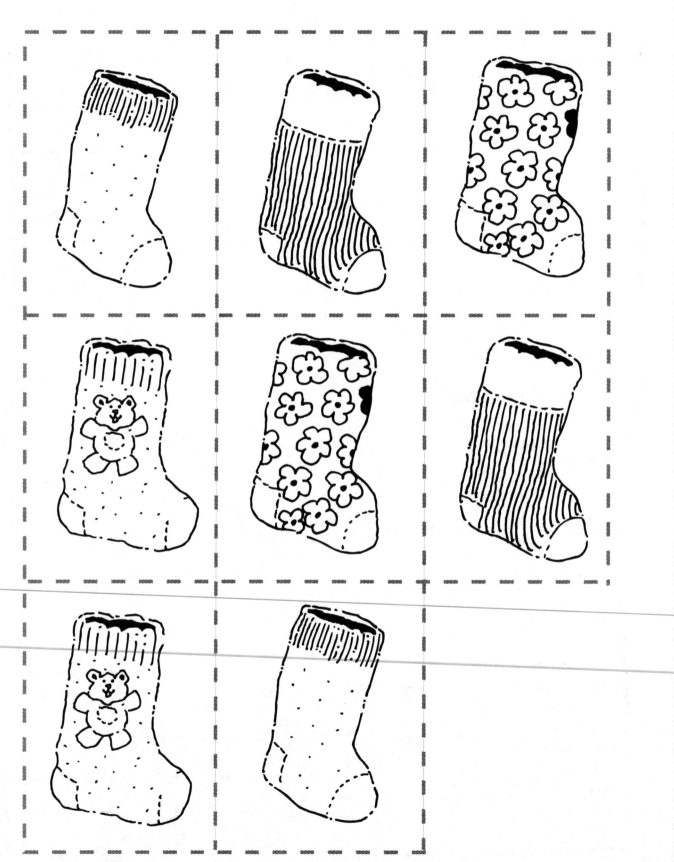

Note: Reproduce this page to use with "A Special Number Line" on page 88.

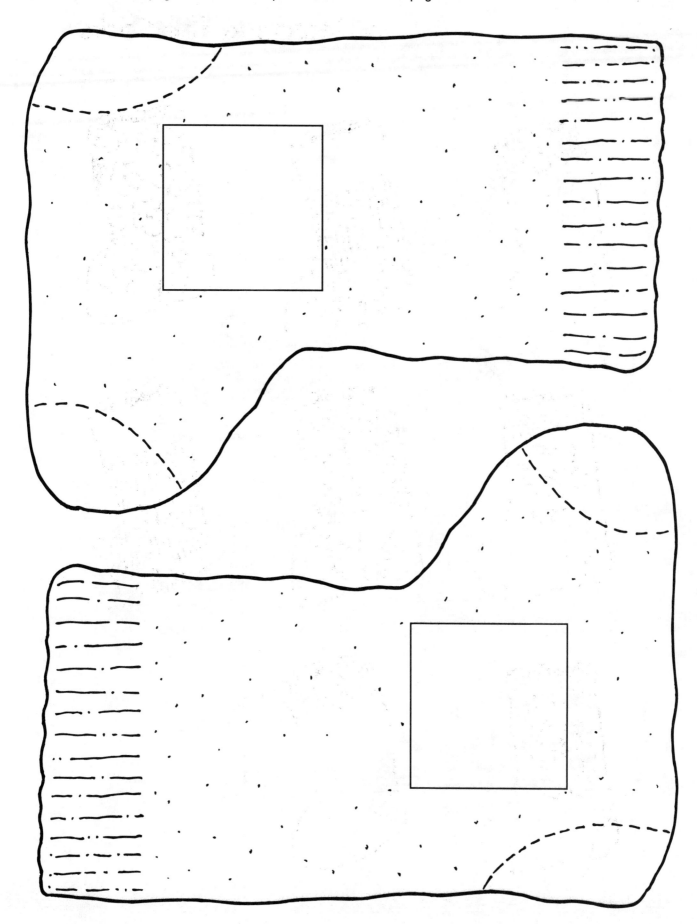

Note: Reproduce these shoes to use with the shoe activities on page 89.

Real Math for Young Learners • EMC 744

Note: Reproduce these shoes to use with the shoe activities on page 89.

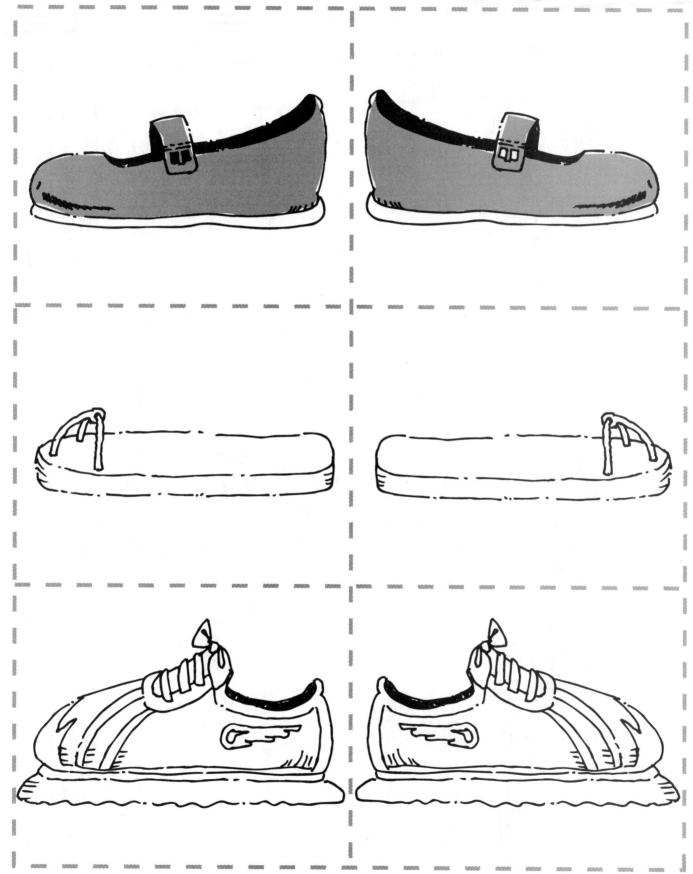

Note: Reproduce these shoes to use with the shoe activities on page 89.

 # Biggest Shoes

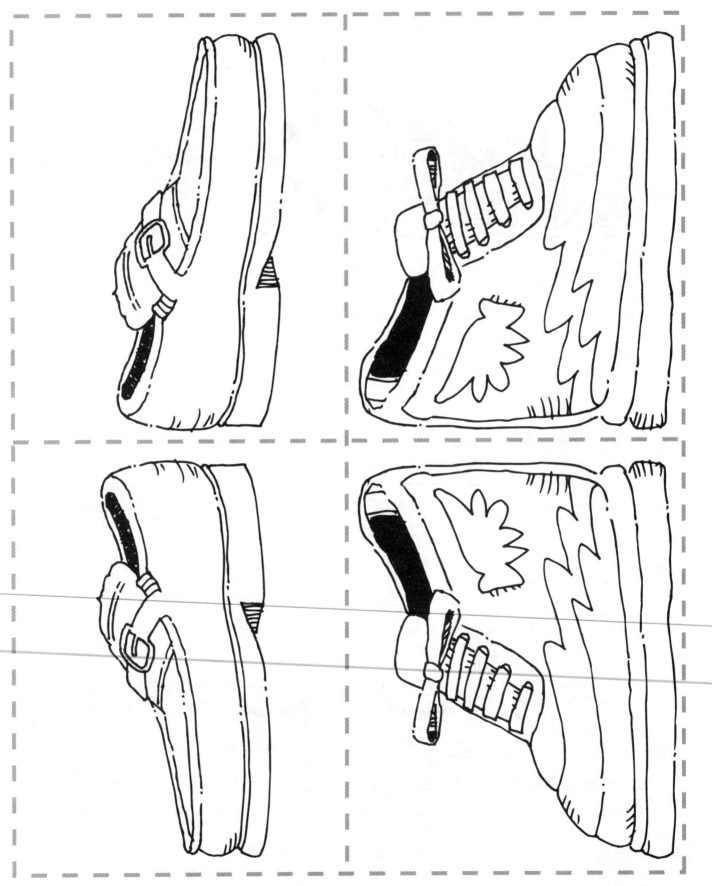

Three Monsters

big

biggest

little

Math Skills: graphing, geometric shapes, patterning

 # Baubles and Beads

Classify and Graph

Wear as many pieces of jewelry as you can, including several items in each category that you want to discuss. Have your students graph the jewelry that you are wearing in a real graph. Begin by asking students to name the different kinds of jewelry that you are wearing. Label columns of the floor grid with these categories. Lay one piece of jewelry in a square in the appropriate column.

Have students interpret the graph by telling or writing their observations.

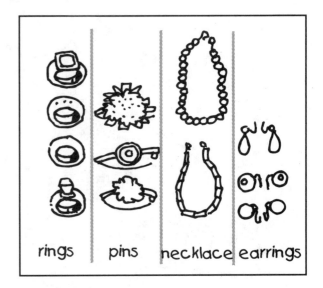

rings   pins   necklace   earrings

Geometry and Jewels

Show pieces of jewelry that represent different geometric shapes. Identify the shapes with the class. Reproduce page 97 and have students complete the page independently to show that they recognize different geometric shapes.

   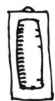

A Pattern in a Necklace

1. Show the class a real necklace that has a repeating pattern. Challenge students to make their own pattern necklaces.

2. Set up a pattern station with bowls of colored loop cereal or several kinds of macaroni. Provide lengths of string or yarn attached to a pipe cleaner. Make the strings two feet long to allow for tying the completed necklace. Tie a piece of the cereal to the end of the string to form a "knot."

   Students string cereal or macaroni to make a pattern.

3. Take the time to have students read and classify their patterns. Here is another graphing opportunity.

   • How many necklaces have an ABAB pattern?

   • How many have an AABAAB pattern?

   Use the floor grid to make this real graph.

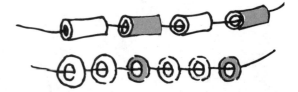

My name is _____ .

Identify the Shapes

Draw a line to match the jewelry and the shape.

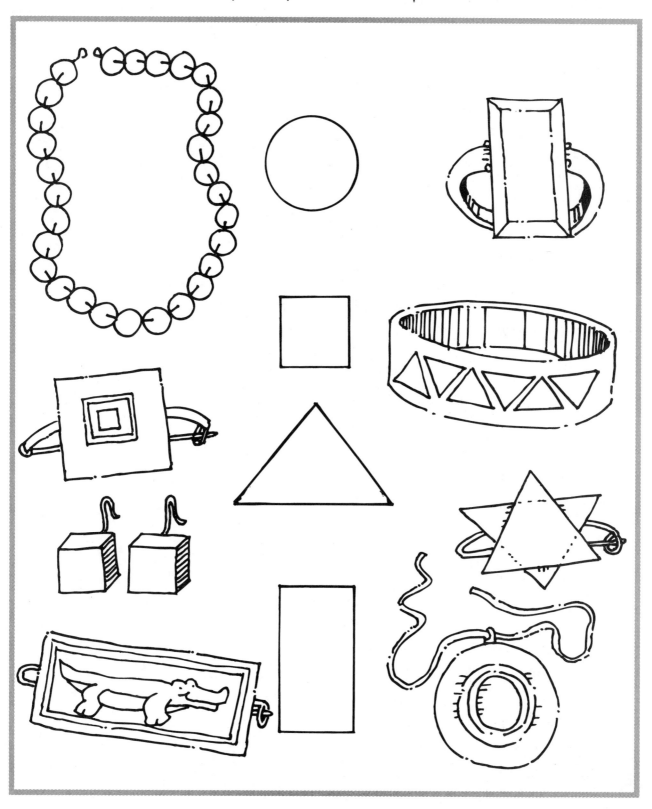

Mittens and Gloves

Building Patterns

1. Show your class several pairs of mittens and several pairs of gloves. Have them describe the differences and the similarities.

   Be sure to note that gloves have places for fingers.

2. Reproduce, color, and cut out a number of copies of the gloves and mittens on pages 99 and 100. Use them to make a pattern. Begin with a simple mitten, glove, mitten, glove. Have students read and name the patterns (ABAB, etc.). Include a difficult one that uses an attribute such as color to challenge good patterners.

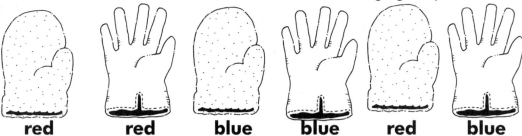

red   **red**   **blue**   **blue**   **red**   **blue**

Counting by Fives

1. Reproduce five copies of the gloves on page 100.

2. Use a group of gloves to help students count by fives. Begin by counting all of the fingers.

   1 , 2 , 3 , 4, 5   Write 5 on the palm of the glove.

   6 , 7 , 8 , 9, 10   Write 10 on the palm of the glove.

   11,12, 13,14, 15   Write 15 on the palm of the glove.

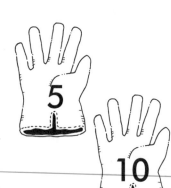

   Continue to 100 or a number appropriate to your group.

3. Have students tell how many fingers by reading only the palm numbers.

4. Post the gloves for easy reference.

Note: Reproduce this page to use with "Building Patterns" on page 98.

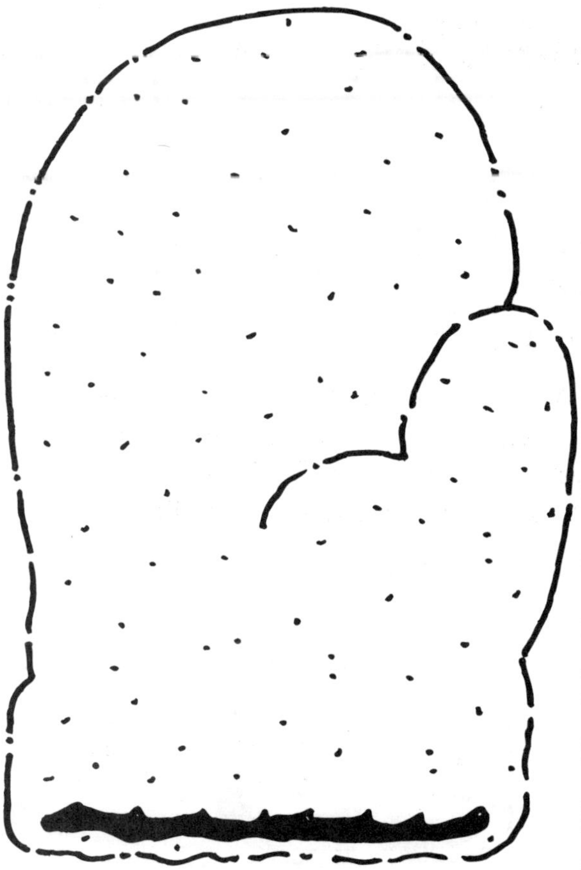

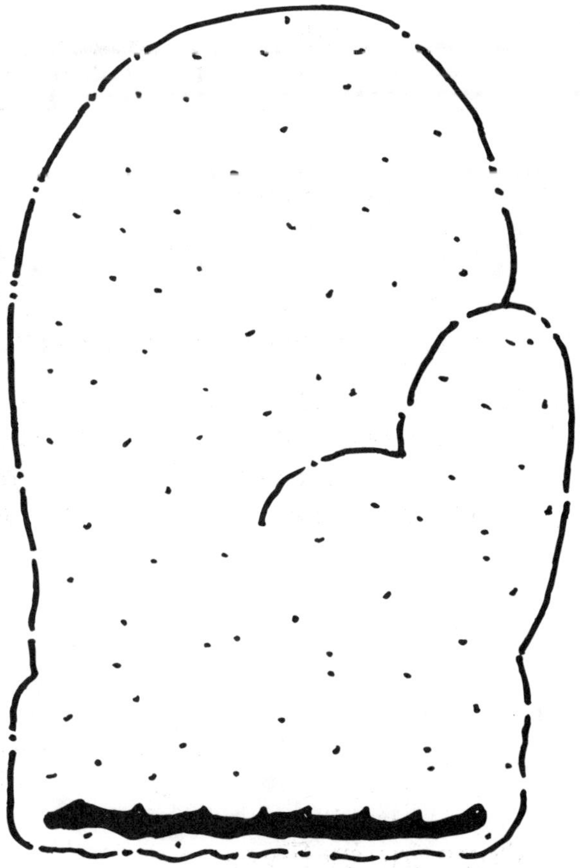

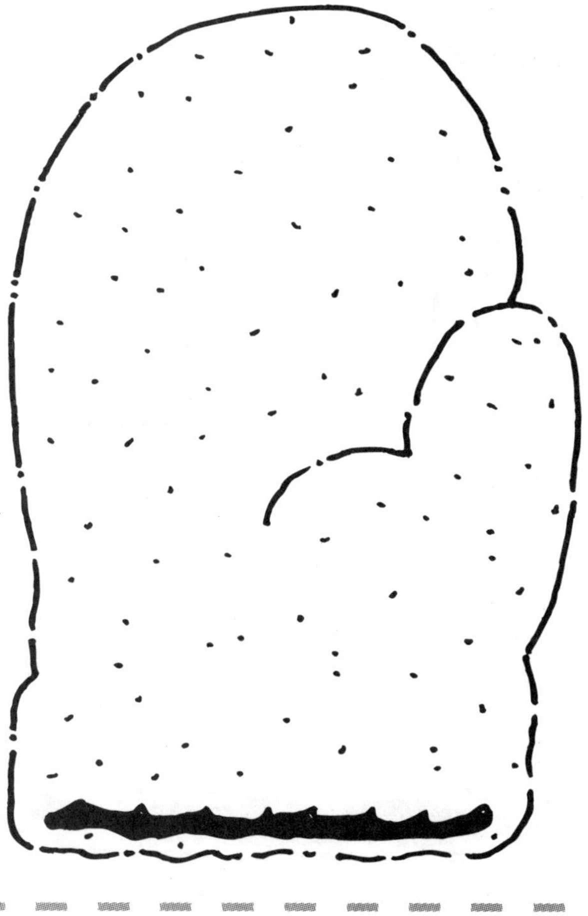

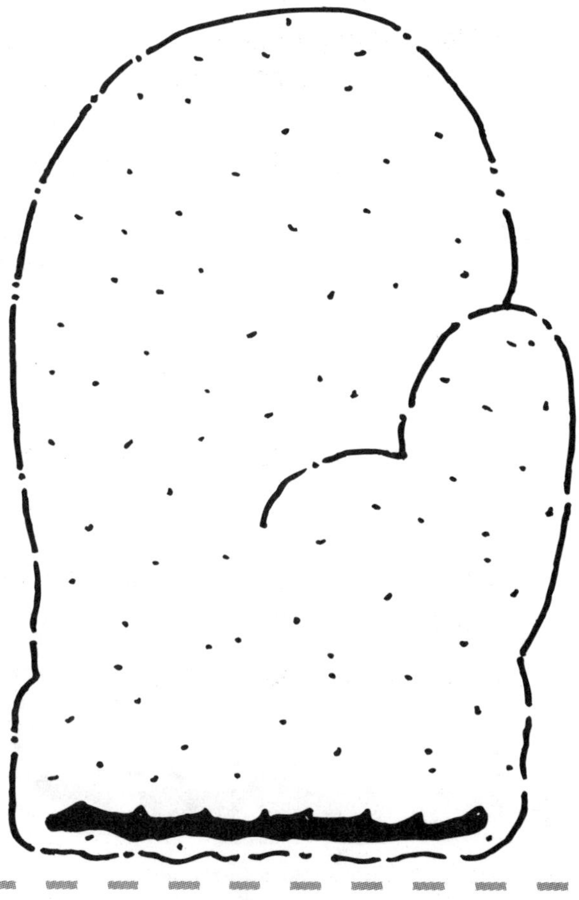

Real Math for Young Learners • EMC 744

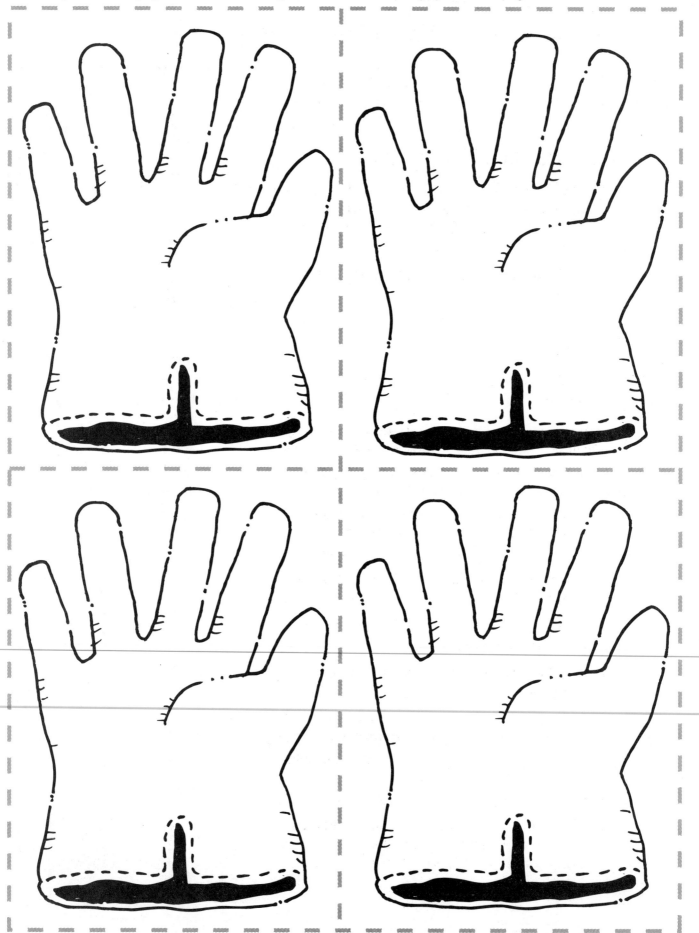

What's in the Closet?

Play this game to practice identifying mathematical attributes.

Before You Begin

To make your "closet," attach a poster board "door" to a bulletin board or flannel board. You will open the door to reveal what is in the closet. Sets of items are provided on pages 103-106.

Collect additional pictures or use real items to represent things in your closet.

How to Start

The object of the game is to identify the "closet rule" after viewing the items.

1. Put one of the sets provided or a category of items you have collected behind the closet door.

2. Open the door to the closet and show the things inside to the class. Say, "All the things in this closet are alike in some way. Can you tell me how they are alike?" Allow students to suggest attributes. As guesses are made, check them. For example:

   > Student: "I think all the things in the closet have two buttons."

   > Teacher: "Count the buttons on each thing to see if the guess is correct."

3. Explain that the *Rule of the Closet* is the thing that is alike about each item in the closet.

   When the rule has been identified, take several new items, show them to the class, and ask if they could go in the closet. Students will check to see if they follow the closet's rule and decide whether they can be put inside.

4. Change the items inside and work with students to discover the new closet's rule. Continue until students are comfortable with the procedure.

Extend the game by creating a closet big book.

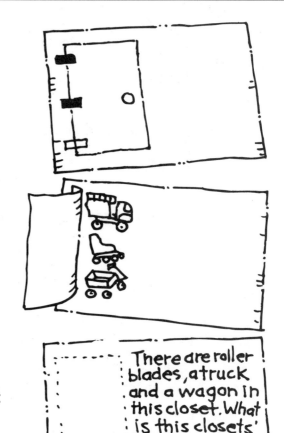

1. Reproduce the closet door pattern on page 107 for each student.

2. Have students decorate their doors and then staple left side of the door to a 12" x 18" (30.5 x 45.5 cm) sheet of construction paper.

3. Behind their doors, students draw several items that follow a rule.

4. The text on the page can be written by the student or the teacher and should tell what items are in the closet. For example: There are boots, socks, shoes, mittens, and skates in this closet. What is this closet's "rule"? The rule can be written on the back of the page. For example: Things that come in pairs belong in this closet.

5. Allow time for students to share their pages with the class and for the class to guess the closets' rules. Bind the pages into a class big book. The cover should give readers directions for enjoying the book. You might want to write them inside a closet door on the cover.

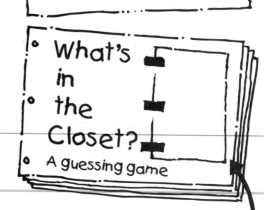

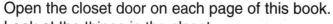

Open the closet door on each page of this book.
Look at the things in the closet.
Try to find out something that is the same about all of the things.
Then guess the rule for putting things in that closet.

Note: Reproduce these sets to use as examples for the game "What's in the Closet?" on page 101.

Note: Reproduce these sets to use as examples for the game "What's in the Closet?" on page 101.

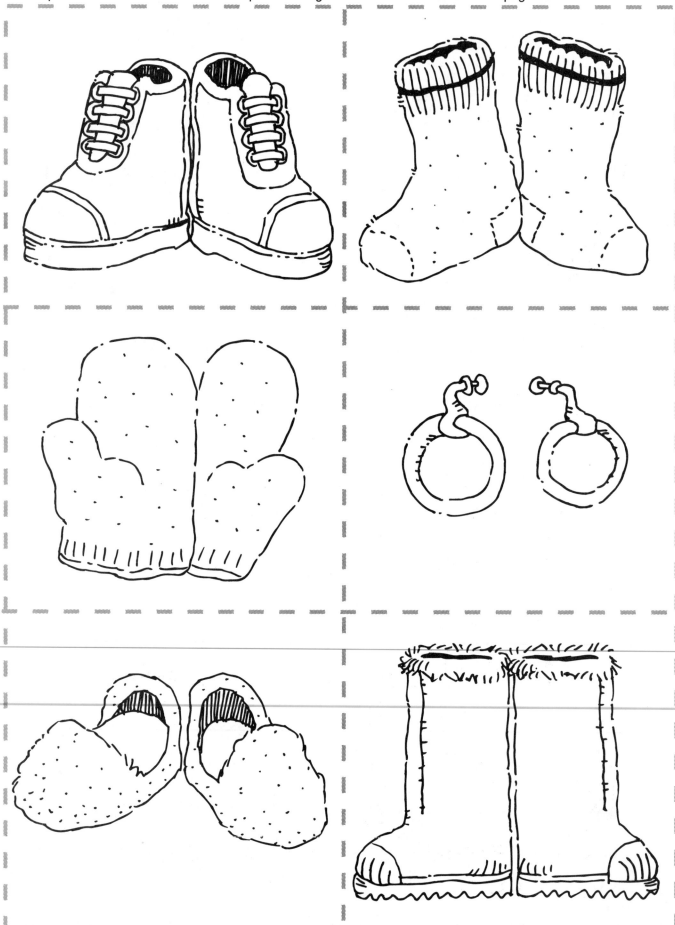

105

Note: Reproduce these sets to use as examples for the game "What's in the Closet?" on page 101.

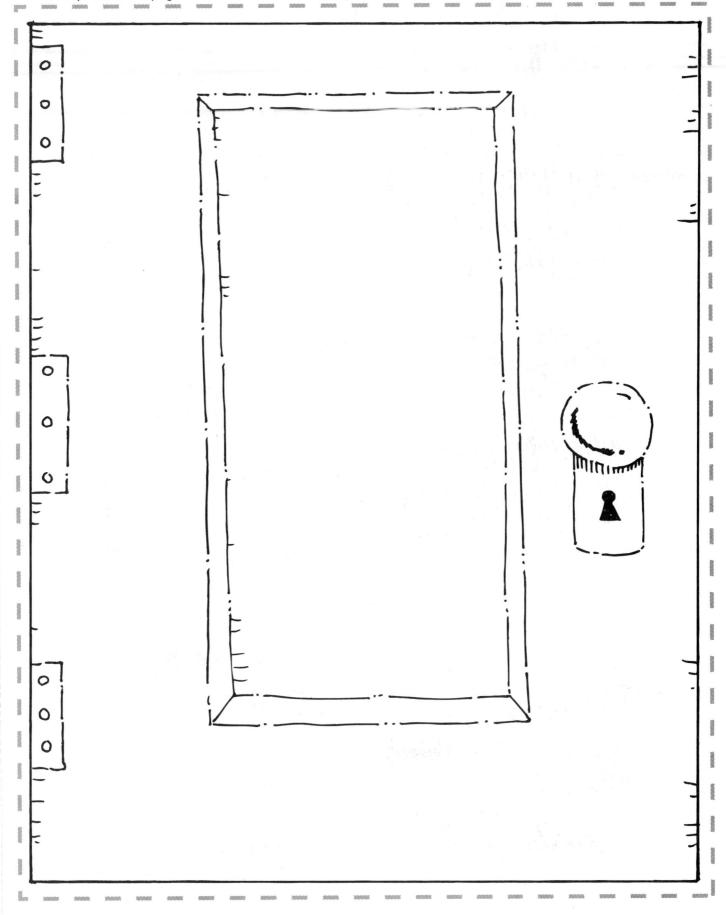

★ Counting in the Closet ★

1. Use the large closet door you made for "What's in the Closet?" on page 101. Fold it along one side to make a hinge. Staple the hinged part to a bulletin board. Make several copies of the patterns on page 109. Make cards containing the symbols +, -, =.

What's in the closet?

2. Place several pieces of two types of clothing "in the closet." Select a child to open the door. Ask children to name the clothing they see. Have them count each type of clothing. Write the numeral on the chalkboard or a sheet of chart paper. Then have them count all the clothing to get a total for all of the clothing in the closet.

Tell your students that you are going to make a number sentence with the clothing pictures. Add the symbols + and = in the correct places to create an equation, then how to read this number "sentence."

 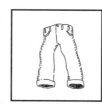

$2 + 1 = 3$

3. Place several items of the same type of clothing in the closet. Have children count how many are in the closet. Write the number on the chalkboard or a chart. Select a child to remove some clothes, telling you how many he/she is taking away. Write this number. Ask the class to count how many are left and write the number down. Add the - and = signs and show children how to read this subtraction sentence.

$4 - 2 = 2$

Note: Reproduce this page to use with the activity on page 108.

Important Numbers

Numbers at Home

We use many numbers to keep track of our day, to plan the future, to keep in contact with others. Have students think of numbers that are important for them to know. Guide them with questions and comments to create a list of these numbers. Discuss why each is important to know. For example:

It is important to know my telephone number at home.

It is important to know how much lunch costs.

It is important to know my birthday.

It is important to know 911.

It is important to know my address.

It is important to know what size clothes I wear.

It is important to know my Mother's work number.

Reproduce the "important numbers" booklet on page 111 for each child. Have children cut the pages apart and staple together to make the booklets, then take them home to fill in with their parents.

Note: Reproduce this form to use with the activity on page 110.

Important Telephone Numbers

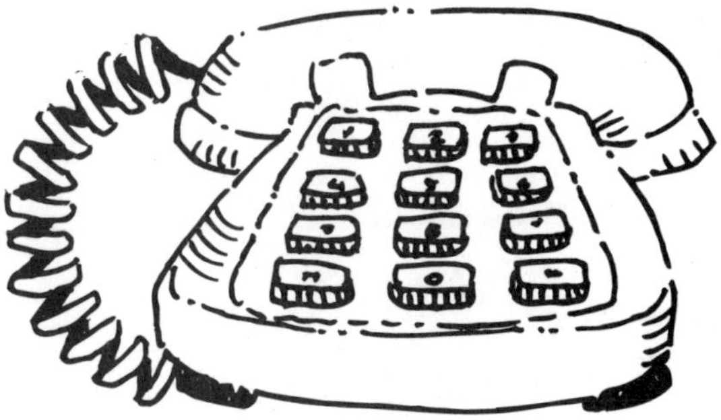

Emergency Telephone Numbers

911

My Friends' Telephone Numbers

Birthdays

Bibliography

At the Laundromat by Christine Lomis; Scholastic, 1993

Belinda's New Spring Hat by Eleanor Clymer; Franklin Watts, 1969.

Bird's New Shoes by Chris Riddell; Henry Holt & Company, 1987.

The Button Book by Margarette S. Reid; Puffin Unicorn, 1990.

Caps for Sale by Esphyr Slobodkina; Harper & Row, 1968.

Coping with Food Trash by Jamie Daniel and Veronica Bonar; Gareth Stevens, 1994.

Cup Cooking: Individual Child Portions Picture Recipes by Barbara Johnson; Early Educators, 1990.

Daddy Makes the Best Spaghetti by Anna Hines; Houghton Mifflin, 1988.

The Emperor's New Clothes retold by Riki Levinson; Dutton's Children's Books, 1991.

Games by Rose Griffiths; Gareth Stevens, 1994.

I Can Make It! Fun Food by Sara Lynn; Bantam, 1994.

The Kitchen by Bobbie Kilman; Crabtree Publishing Company, 1990.

Kitchen Fun: A Cookbook for Kids by Lois P. Bell; Random House, 1988.

Kitchen Fun: A Hearty Helping of Things to Make, Play, and Eat by Beth Murray; Boyd Mills Press, 1994.

The Mitten Tree by Candance Christiansen; Putnam Publishing Group, 1995.

My Cake (First Step Science) by Sheila Gore; Gareth Stevens, 1995.

My Two Feet by Alice Schertle; Lothrop, Lee & Shepard Books, 1985.

Numbers by Rose Griffiths; Gareth Stevens, 1994.

One, Two, One Pair by Bruce McMillan; Scholastic, 1991.

Polka Dots, Checks, and Stripes by Carol Cornelius; Children's Press, 1978.

The Principal's New Clothes by Stephanie Calmenson; Scholastic, 1989.

Shoes From Grandpa by Mem Fox; Orchard Books, 1989.

The Socksnatchers by Lorna Balian; Abingdon Press, 1988.

Take Time to Relax by Nancy Carlson; Viking, 1991.

Ten in a Bed by Allen Ahlberg; Viking Kestrel, 1989.

10 Bears in My Bed—A Goodnight Countdown by Stan Mack; Pantheon Books, 1974.

This Is a House by Colleen Bare; Cobblehill Books/Dutton, 1992.

The Winter Mittens by Tim Arnold; Margaret K. McElderry Books, 1988.

Try On a Shoe by Jane Belk Moncure; The Child's World, 1973.

Two Little Shoes by Razvan; Bradbury Press, 1993.

Where Does This Come From? by H.I. Peeples; Contemporary Books, 1989.

Where Oh Where Is My Underwear? by Barney Saltzberg; Hyperion Books for Children, 1994.

Whose Shoes Are These? by Ron Roy; Clarion Books, 1988.

A World of Shoes by Della Rowland; Contemporary Books, Inc., 1989.